Also by JILL KREMENTZ

How It Feels to Live with a Physical Disability

Jill Krementz

SIMON & SCHUSTER

NEW YORK   LONDON   TORONTO   SYDNEY   TOKYO   SINGAPORE

SIMON & SCHUSTER
Simon & Schuster Building
Rockefeller Center
1230 Avenue of the Americas
New York, New York 10020

Book design by Barbara Marks; layout by Jill Krementz
Manufactured in the United States of America

3   5   7   9   10   8   6   4

Library of Congress Cataloging-in-Publication data

Krementz, Jill
How it feels to live with a physical disability / Jill Krementz.
p.   cm.
1. Physically handicapped children—United States—Biography—
Juvenile literature.   2. Physically handicapped children—United
States—Psychology—Case studies—Juvenile literature.   I. Title.
HV904.K74   1992
362.4′083—dc20   91-43335
                                                             CIP

ISBN: 0-671-72371-5

This book is dedicated with love and thanks
to
James D. Wolfensohn

I am deeply grateful for a generous grant
from the Botwinick-Wolfensohn Foundation
and the extent to which it made this
project possible.

I am equally indebted to Jim Dettre, Tom
Dimuzio, Dorothy Matsu, and Bonnie Petrauskas
at Johnson & Johnson Consumer Products. This
wonderful company has supported my work and
donated copies of my books to thousands of
health care professionals throughout the United
States.

Contents

Preface

FOR MANY PEOPLE THE only contact they have with the disabled or handicapped is a quick glance in their direction and a sense of embarrassment which makes them look away. Although I have been involved in the care of children with disabilities since my days in medical school, I still cannot explain this phenomenon. An element exists in human nature which somehow distrusts or is repelled by physical incongruities in others. Jill Krementz in this thoughtful and caring book has achieved three important goals. First, she allows the reader to see beyond the physical disability, to recognize the human being who also may have an absent leg, a twisted arm, a deformed face, or who is blind. Second, she allows all the children to describe in their own way how it feels to have a physical disability and the negative and positive effects upon them from others, including parents, brothers and sisters, friends, and teachers. And finally, the stories the children tell allow us to recognize not only the strength of the human spirit and how it can overcome vast hurdles but also how it needs to be loved and nourished.

Two quotes from these stories are particularly telling and poignant:

"We're all in the same boat." Who among us has not had our own self-doubts?

"Hi, I'm me and this is the way I am." Is that not the goal we all seek—acceptance of ourselves by ourselves and by others?

Jill Krementz has captured all of this in the words of the children and in her expressive photographs. The readers of her book will come away with a better understanding of what it means to have a physical disability and a deeper appreciation of what these young people have to overcome in order to establish their own independence and sense of worth. Their remarkable achievements are an inspiration to all of us.

LEON ROOT, M.D.
Chief of Pediatric Orthopedics
Hospital for Special Surgery in New York City

Introduction

WE USE A NUMBER of terms to describe those whose bodies are not perfectly formed: congenitally defective, physically impaired, handicapped, disadvantaged, disabled. I don't really like any of them because they imply negative attributes, something that is lacking or cannot be done. I prefer to think of the young people who tell their stories in this book as merely different—as diverse in their individual ways as we all are. They may not look like other children, or they may not be able to do all the things other children can do. But their circumstances have led them to develop many very positive attributes and unique abilities both of body and mind.

These children, first of all, have extraordinary courage. Confronting their physical differences with complete honesty, they are determined to challenge those limits, to learn, to grow, to live their lives to the fullest. Emotionally, they have an inner strength that has enabled them to fight and to keep fighting until they triumph over the odds against them. They have devised ingenious ways to conquer an environment that is often hostile, both in the physical dexterity and psychic energy it demands, and in the attitudes people have toward those who may lack these skills. Above all, they do not feel sorry for themselves, and they do not want us to feel sorry for them either.

In writing the stories of these remarkable role models and photographing them for this book, I was, as we all are, first drawn to their differences. But I soon discovered a special quality they all shared. I can only describe it as beauty, a kind of beauty of spirit that informs their words, their actions, even their faces. In this way, too, they may be different from those of us who have not had to deal with such pain and adversity. But it is an admirable difference and one that I hope will serve as an inspiration to other children who are physically challenged, as well as their families, and all those who love and work with them. It is a difference that should inspire all of us.

—Jill Krementz

A person who is severely impaired

never knows his hidden sources

of strength until he is treated like a

normal human being and encouraged

to shape his own life.

—HELEN KELLER—

Eli Abarbanel-Wolff

AGE TWELVE

WHEN I WAS BORN, there was nothing physically wrong with me. When I was a year and a half, the doctors found a small hole in my heart which needed to be repaired. I had my operation in 1979, just before my second birthday. The operation was a success, but four days later there were some complications and the doctors said I had had a stroke. A stroke is a sudden loss of sensation and motion caused by the rupture or an obstruction of an artery of the brain. No one is exactly sure why I had this stroke. The event was very traumatic to me and my family.

I had to stay in the hospital a few extra days and I had my second birthday there. When I went home, I couldn't sit or walk and I had a big scar from my surgery. My entire left side was paralyzed. Ten days later I was walking again and the doctors thought everything would be OK, but my left arm remained weak and moved in an awkward, jerky way. In medical terms, my arm would be referred to as spastic. When I got tired, my left leg would drag a bit so I limped, and that's the way it still is.

About a year after my stroke, I started to realize the things I was able and not able to do. The period between ages three and four was very experimental. When I tried to play a sport or physical game, I would try to do what my friends could do. I would keep on trying even though it was impossible for me to keep up with them because I did not understand the limits of what I could do. For example, when I played catch with my friends, I could barely throw the ball five feet ahead of me. But my friends were able to throw the ball twice as far. I didn't realize why I wasn't able to throw the ball as far as my friends could, so I became very frustrated at my performance. I wasn't aware of the difference between me and my friends. I couldn't walk straight and I stumbled a lot.

When I finally realized what I was and wasn't able to do, I became very depressed. I thought that because of my stroke I would never be able to do anything physical again. I felt worse than the situation really was. Usually at recess my friends would climb on the jungle gym outside in the playground. I would sit inside and watch my friends play, and I felt awful. When my friends asked me to come out and play with them, I told them I couldn't. I was afraid I would fall off the jungle gym if I tried. My friends and family helped me overcome my fears. They encouraged me to try everything, even if I was determined that I couldn't. My friends told me they would watch me so that I wouldn't fall. They helped me change and feel more confident about what I could do.

Usually at a young age, most physically handicapped people realize what they can and cannot do with their handicap. Many go through phases before they reach an understanding of their limits. In my opinion, there is an order to the emotional phases that a person goes through. At first, physically handicapped people aren't aware of why they are different. Then, as they realize it, they become frustrated by their limitations. Soon they become depressed. Then, there is usually an influential friend or parent who helps them get out of their depression and makes them feel better about themselves. These are the first important steps that a young disabled person goes through.

Between ages five and eight, I realized what was wrong with me and why I got to be the way I am. At first I asked a lot of questions, like "Why did this have to happen to me?" "Why was I the one the doctors screwed up on and why don't we sue?" and "Am I deformed?" My parents weren't sure whether to answer my questions completely or not because they didn't think I would understand their answers. But once they had answered my questions, I started to get a better idea of what was wrong, and why it happened.

I also had my own thoughts about what was wrong with me. My imagination was very vivid and active. Sometimes I thought of myself as crippled and condemned to a wheelchair forever. I started thinking that there was no point in living, that I wouldn't be able to contribute to the world, so I might as well die. Other times I imagined a big, mean-looking doctor who pulled out a long, pointed scalpel and started cutting open my chest. Then the doctor's scalpel suddenly slipped and I was different for the rest of my life. But today, I know that it was only an accident.

Also, between the ages of five and eight my temper was very short. I wanted to be accepted as one of the guys and I got angry whenever anybody made fun of me. Another reason for my anger was the stupid accident which made my life so much harder than everybody else's. My brother could easily hit a baseball while I could barely even get my hands on the bat. Sometimes he forgot what had happened to me and teased me about it so I would get mad. And sometimes I would make a stupid mistake, as everyone does. But I would become ashamed and angry at myself. I sometimes hit my arm. During my tantrums I would scream my real and imaginary thoughts about my arm.

After my attack of anger, I would either run away or tell people that I was with to leave. But usually my friends or family would stay with me to the end of my temper tantrum. Eventually I would calm down and turn back to my regular self. At this time my friends and family were very important to me, because they made me realize that I was really perfectly OK the way I was.

All physically handicapped people do things which are clumsy physically, like tripping, or making a dumb play in a game. When they do, they blame it on their handicap. Usually, after they do something clumsy, they feel embarrassed or stupid and they want to be left alone. Another typical response is to walk away from the event and pretend it didn't happen. Instead the person should say, "Next time I'm going to try to remember that everybody makes mistakes." Sometimes my handicap helps make me a better person. I shouldn't blame everything I do wrong on my problem. But even though I try to give myself this little speech when I have a problem, I still get angry at myself. But that's the way I am. My friends usually are there to help calm me down, and I am grateful to them for that.

There are other people who make fun of handicapped people when they stumble or do something clumsy. These people have their own problems. Almost everyone has been laughed at some time in their life. These same people should think before they tease someone else, because they might be laughed at themselves some other time. People who mock and tease others have their own handicaps.

By the time I was ten or eleven, I was totally aware of what I had been through. And sometimes I felt proud of myself for living through all the difficult times. Then I thought I deserved a trophy.

But now I know that I am not the only person with problems and that other people have gone through more serious difficulties than I have, such as being shot, having AIDS, or being burned. I think that every handicapped person who has lived a tough life and accomplished something deserves a trophy, not just me.

Also, during the last few years I have sometimes become more violent when I am mad at myself. Occasionally, I have wanted to kill myself. I have been so frustrated that I thought I wasn't good enough to be alive. Other times I have run out of my house or yelled or hit my arm. But now I have gotten over my most violent phases, and when I do get angry I try to talk to someone about it. My mom is a wonderful listener. She's always there for me when I've got something on my mind.

These were the types of things I went through when I was ten or eleven. I think that most people with handicaps experience many of the same reactions. For example, most of us go through a period when we feel uncomfortable and want to run away or hurt ourselves. But some of us adjust more slowly. It's not just people with handicaps who go through phases. It's everyone. I think it's part of growing up.

When you have a disability, one of the most important issues is knowing when you need help. The reason a person with a handicap doesn't like to ask for help is because he or she is afraid that the person they ask will tease or mock them and will tell people. Why do people laugh at a disability? I'm not sure, but I think it is because at our age most people have their own problems inside, but since someone like me has an obvious problem, he or she is the easiest target.

The first time I needed help from a friend, I was scared and embarrassed to ask for it. I was at school and rushing to get to my next class when my shoelace became untied. When my friend Scott offered to give me a hand, I told him everything was OK and that he should run along. But he persisted, saying, "Are you sure you don't need some help?" I said, "It's OK. I can do it myself. I don't need your help or anybody else's. I need the practice. Besides, I'm afraid the other kids will make fun of me if they see I can't tie my own shoe." At that point Scott said, "I can tell by your temper you need some help tying your shoelaces. I don't want you to trip, and I don't want you to be late for your class. I'm just trying to be a friend," and he knelt down and started to help.

Once my friend helped me, I wasn't scared anymore and then I felt I could ask for help more often. These kinds of incidents have helped me to overcome the scary feelings. My friends have been a big help to me. All people with disabilities—and without— need friends who will treat them with respect, will not make them feel foolish, and will help them when they need it.

My friends and family have made me the person I am today. When I am frustrated, they make me feel better. And when I have accomplished something important, they congratulate me and make me feel good. When I need help in doing something, they are always there to help out. They have always pushed me further to reach whatever goal I have set for myself.

This past year I gave some assemblies at my school so that everyone would have more understanding of what it's like to have a physical disability. The first assembly I gave was for the students and teachers, but the parents heard about it and so I put on a special meeting in

the evening for all of them. After I had talked about what it was like to have a disability, I asked for volunteers from the audience to come up on the stage. I told them we would participate in two activities. One would be tying a shoelace and the other would be peeling an orange. Both of these activities would be done with one hand. I explained that these were two things that even I, with all my practice, couldn't do perfectly or without a certain amount of frustration. The two main requisites are practice and co-ordination.

I spoke to some of the participants later. Mrs. Wineburg, a teacher at my school, said that she couldn't even count the number of oranges she had eaten in her lifetime and that it certainly took a lot more time to peel an orange with one hand. She said that she had seen my tantrums when I was younger but had never understood the depth of my anger until that assembly. She was in tears.

Mr. Sachse, the father of one of my classmates, volunteered for one-handed shoelace tying. What he said is "It took a lot more *thinking* than I realized, a lot of planning, and in the end my shoelaces weren't as tight as they should have been." He said it was the first time anyone with a handicap had explained to him, step by step, how it felt—that he had never understood the various stages. He admitted that he still had just as much apprehension about whether or not he should help a person with a handicap or whether he would be interfering, but he congratulated me on what he called "a spectacular presentation." He also told me about an excellent piece in *The New Yorker* magazine about Sir Jeffrey Tate, a British conductor who was born with spina bifida.

I think that people who don't have physical disabilities have a hard time realizing how much psychic energy gets used up by those who have them. They realize that people like myself might have trouble with sports, but it's the day-to-day tasks that can defeat you. I think the two experiments at my assembly helped my friends understand more about what my daily life is like and how frustrating it can be.

I have not had the easiest life, but in some ways it has made me a better person. Now I realize what other people with physical handicaps go through and what they feel. Also, I am more aware of other people's faults because that is something I can relate to and accept. And sometimes I feel my personality has changed, too, because of my stroke. Some people tell me, "You're so nice. I wonder if it had anything to do with your stroke." It's hard to know why I'm the way I am. It's true that I usually like being helpful to my friends and my family. These things are a part of my personality. I hope these traits *will* stay until the end of my life.

This year I feel as though I have changed a lot and have had some major accomplishments. Besides the school assembly presentation, I have found new ways to do things that I haven't been able to do in the past. For example, in tennis I have developed a one-handed serve.

Also I've been learning how to use biofeedback, which is a kind of therapy used to relax tense muscles. Once a week I have biofeedback training with Karen Kverno and Cindy Pearlman at the Medical Illness Counseling Center. It's basically a tool to help me regain more functional use of my affected arm and leg. My main problem is not that my arm and leg are too weak but that I have too much muscle activity on my left side. That prevents normal movement and also causes spasms which can be uncomfortable.

The way it works is that I sit in a comfortable chair and electrodes

are placed on certain muscles. Cindy, who is my physical therapist,
helps me with certain muscular movements while Karen interprets
the visual and audio feedback. Karen has taught me how to relax
my whole body. I've also learned from Cindy how to relax specific
muscle groups while activating others. I can watch the muscle spasm
activity in my arm on a monitor. When the lines are all jagged, it
means there's a lot of muscle activity. When I relax certain muscles,
I can see a straight line on the screen. Since it's often hard for me
to feel my muscles, it helps when I can see the muscle activity and

then try to control it. Cindy and Karen are a great team and we have a pretty good time.

I've been doing biofeedback off and on for about five years. My goal is to be able to relax my muscles at will without having to rely on the biofeedback instrument. Learning to relax has been a big help to me before important sports events or when I've been preparing for a big exam in school. And the neuromuscular reeducation has helped me with functional skills, such as holding down a piece of paper with my left hand when I'm writing on it. Luckily, I'm right-handed. It's also helped me with my balance, which allows me to walk without tripping and to play center forward on the school soccer team! Last year I had the most assists and was voted one of the most valuable players. Being able to participate in sports has made me more confident about myself. When I step out onto the field, I feel as though I'm stepping into a dream where I forget all my problems. I feel like a person without any worries.

Ivonne Mosquera

AGE THIRTEEN

I DON'T EVER REMEMBER seeing—what colors look like, or people, or anything. I was born in South America. I was living in Colombia with my parents and two older sisters, Sandra and Liliana, when I was diagnosed as having retina blastoma bilateral, which means cancerous tumors in my eyes. I was fifteen months old. My family moved to the United States a month later, just before I had the operation to remove my left eye. The doctors took out my right eye about six months later. If they hadn't removed my eyes, the cancer would have spread to my brain and killed me.

After the operations were finished, my parents decided we should stay in America. They felt that people with handicaps have more opportunities here. My parents have always taught me that blind people can do anything sighted people can do. They enrolled me in P.S. 6 in New York, a regular public school, when I was in kindergarten. Putting a person with a disability in a regular school is called mainstreaming.

At first, when I was teased for being blind, I wanted to be in a special class. Nobody else understood how being blind feels. But after a while, I got used to the kids in my class and they got used to me. Now I feel good about school because I'm learning everything I can possibly learn, and because I have a lot of friends.

When I was in nursery school, a long time ago, I learned braille. Braille is an alphabet for the blind. Letters, numbers, and symbols are made up of combinations of raised dots. I can read by running my fingers over the dots. There is a special machine like a typewriter that allows me to write braille. I have one at home and one at school, so I can take notes and do homework like other kids. All my school books and a lot of the games I have at home are in braille, too. One good thing about braille is that hardly anybody can read it, so you can write whatever you want in your diary and know that secrets will be safe.

Every morning, a special teacher comes to my school for an hour to help me with questions I have and to put my braille into print so that my regular classroom teacher can check my work. My best subjects are math, Spanish, and English. My worst is social studies. Art doesn't have any meaning for me. I think someday I'd like to be a math teacher.

Outside of school, I take lots of different kinds of instruction. Mobility lessons are very important. A special instructor from the Board of Education teaches me to get around by myself on the street. Part of it is learning to use a cane, but mostly it's learning to develop my hearing as my main tool of guidance. You have to block out all the other noises on the street and listen to the traffic. People are always offering to help me cross, but I try to figure out for myself when it's safe to walk without help. I used to think, "Why don't people mind their own business?" Now I realize they are being nice, and that it means they care. If I really do need a hand, I can ask for it. I am also learning to use a laser cane. I think it's fun. The laser cane is great because with a regular cane, you don't know there's an obstacle in front of you until you're right on top of it. The laser cane senses objects when they are five feet away and lets you know through a series of vibrations. That way you can avoid obstacles better.

Sometimes I feel a little embarrassed when I walk on the street with my cane. When I'm at home, or in school, I can get around quickly without any help, so I don't like people in my neighborhood seeing me with the cane. I don't want them to feel sorry for me. Usually I go places with my family and friends, so I rarely have to use the cane. Still, it's important that I take the lessons and practice a lot, because there will come a time when I'll want or need to go places alone.

I take dance lessons for visually impaired children with Jacques

d'Amboise. I found out about the classes at the Lighthouse for the Blind, which is where my mother works and also where I went to nursery school. I am the only totally blind child in my class—everyone else has some sight. I take both ballet and jazz classes, but I like the ballet better. It has become a part of me. When I have to skip a lesson, I really miss it—it throws off my body's schedule.

I've often thought that I'd like to be a famous dancer, but I know it's a difficult goal to attain. I would always need to have someone there to tell me whether what I was doing was correct and looked right. I think if I pursue being a teacher or a businesswoman, I will be able to get by on my own. No matter what my career is, I always want to keep ballet as a hobby.

Besides dance, I have been taking piano lessons at the Lighthouse with Joseph Fields since I was eight. I'm a little lazy about practicing,

but I think I'm a pretty good player once I get into it. When I feel like it, I'll practice for an hour or maybe a little more, especially if I like the piece I'm learning. We give student recitals four times a year.

Basically, I'm good at taking care of myself. Of course, I have to rely on my mother or my sisters to take me to my lessons, but getting dressed and stuff is not a problem. In the morning, my body acts as my alarm clock, since I'm so used to getting up at the same time every day. I wear prosthetic eyes, which are made out of special plastic and look just like real eyes. They're easy because I only have to take them out and clean them once every week or two.

People ask me if I pick out my own clothes. The answer is yes. I dress myself every morning and do my own hair. Once in a while I'll worry, "Gosh, does what I'm wearing look good?" Then I'll have to ask someone. Usually, I just have to feel that it looks good. I like to look my best because there are a lot of people who think, "She's blind, and that's why she's not matching." Or, "Her family doesn't care" and "They just put any clothes on her." I want people to know that just because I'm blind doesn't mean I'm totally different from them. I feel like a regular person. The only different thing about me is I can't see.

I'm lucky because I have a loving family and friends who don't treat me like I'm different. We play games and go to the mall and even go to the movies together. I'm not at a stage yet where my friends are all dating, so we go out in groups, which is fun. It's good to be with people, because they tell me things that happen that I can't see. In the movies, for example, a lot happens on the screen that doesn't involve sounds.

Sometimes it bothers me that I can't see the way somebody looks.

It usually doesn't help much to ask a sighted person, because I don't know what it means when they say, "That girl is pretty," or "He has brown hair." But in a way it's an advantage that I'm blind, because I don't judge a book by its cover. If I think people are cute, it's usually not because my sisters or friends tell me so, but because of their voice or the way they act.

When I dream at night, I picture people as what I think they look like. They might come into my dreams as a voice, or I might know them by their height or what they are wearing. I don't think the pictures I make in my mind are similar to the pictures a sighted person would make, but I can always tell who the people in my dreams are.

Sometimes I worry about my cancer coming back. I had a friend who also went to nursery school at the Lighthouse. She was a year younger than me. She had the same kind of cancer I did, and also had her eyes removed, but unfortunately, her cancer came back when she was about ten years old. She passed away recently. My doctor tells me there's only a very small chance my cancer will come back, so I try not to think about it a lot.

In the past few years, I have had a lot of problems. First of all, two favorite teachers died. One of them, Mr. Skahill, was my first mobility teacher. He taught me how to use a cane and was the first person with whom I walked outside, independently, without my family or friends. Shortly after he died, Mrs. Joseph died, too. She was my resource room teacher who prepared me to be mainstreamed on a full-time basis. I worked with her for four years, from kindergarten to third grade. Also, my parents split up. They were both very careful to tell my sisters and me that it was just between the two of them, and had nothing to do with us, so I have never worried that my being blind caused it in any way. Despite all the trouble, I know that my parents love me and are proud of me. Also, my mother and sisters are always around to give me a hand whenever I need one.

No matter what happens, I'm determined not to give up. My main message is, even though I'm blind, even though it may take me a bit longer to do certain things, I can still do them. And so could another blind person. Once you accomplish a goal, you'll be the person who feels good about it. Whether or not other people congratulate you for it, you'll feel better, and you'll know that you did it because of you—because you never gave up.

Nathan Yoder

AGE EIGHT

My mom found out that I was a dwarf while she was still in the delivery room. I weighed just as much as an average boy—eight pounds three ounces—but the doctors could tell right away because of the shortness of my limbs. My arms and legs were shorter than they should be. It was lucky that I was born in the Washington/Baltimore area because that's where the people who know the most about dwarfs happen to be. Mommy says if I had been born in Kansas, they might not have picked up on it. My mom and dad are both normal height. So's my older brother Michael.

I first realized I was different when I was in preschool. That's when I started spending a lot of time with other kids my age and they were all bigger than I was. My mom looked at eighteen preschools and picked St. Columba's Nursery School because it included children with special needs, and since it was all on one level, I wouldn't have to go up and down stairs. The school also had a lot of animals, which my mom felt was important. She says if you can relate well to an animal, it will help you get along with your friends.

Mommy calls me a short-statured person, but I usually call myself a short person because it's easier. Some people think I'm a midget but that's because they don't know the difference between a dwarf and a midget. A midget is a miniature person. Everything's smaller than average—head, body, and arms and legs. Some dwarfs, like me, may have a normal-sized head and body with short arms and short legs. I'm thirty-seven inches high—just over three feet—and I weigh forty-two pounds. Lots of dwarfs are bowlegged, and a few have knock-knees because our bones bend a lot. I will probably have to have an operation in a few years to straighten my legs a little. They'll put me to sleep with sleeping gas and when I wake up I'll be able to walk without being pigeon-toed. Mommy has already bought a walker for me at a garage sale and I'll use that for a while after the operation.

My doctor's name is Dr. Kopits, who is at Children's Hospital and Center for Reconstructive Surgery in Baltimore. He's a surgeon who specializes in little people, and he's famous all over the world for his work. I go to see him about once a year, and his waiting room is so crowded with people like me you can hardly find a place to sit down. Dr. Kopits is from Hungary and he's invented a lot of the operations he does on dwarfs. He always gives me a big kiss and a hug whenever I go for a visit. You can tell he really loves his patients. The only part I hate about my yearly checkup is having to sit for so long in the waiting room. We've had to wait for over five hours each time and it makes me mad. Doctors should learn how to schedule their patients better. I had to miss a whole day of school.

I go to a regular school and I'm in the third grade. My friends treat me like everyone else—most of the time. It's the people I don't know who cause problems, like they'll call me "shorty" or "shrimp." When

that happens I get mad at them. I don't cry. When I get really mad I chase them away. Even though they're a lot bigger than I am, they get scared and start running. Sometimes the first graders, or even the kids in kindergarten, make fun of me because I'm smaller than they are. They bug me a lot. If I get too upset, I ask the teacher for help. My main problems are when I'm in places where people don't know me. When I go to a restaurant, they always treat me like a baby. Or if my mom takes me somewhere and I'm walking beside her without holding on to her hand, they think she's a bad mother. That's because they figure I'm only two or three years old.

It helps that I've gone to the same school for a while because my classmates have gotten used to me. When I need help reaching a tray in the cafeteria, whoever's nearby gives me a hand. And my teacher knows I need a stool under my desk to rest my feet on. My legs are too short to reach the floor and it would be bad for my circulation to let them dangle in midair. Besides, after a while my feet would fall asleep and that feels awful. My desk is smaller than the other kids'.

When you're a dwarf, buying clothes that fit can be a real problem. The sleeves and pants legs are always too long. I'm lucky because my grandmother loves to sew and she makes most of my clothes. Mommy measures me all over. I like to stand on the kitchen table

when we do this. Grandma doesn't make my winter coats, so when we buy them we shorten the sleeves ourselves. I need a very wide shoe—EE—and there's only one brand of tennis shoes that fits me. We usually buy these ahead of time if we can so I'll always have a pair to grow into. My grandfather helps in other ways. He's very handy building things, and he made me a special step stool in the bathroom so I could reach the sink more easily. My grandparents both live in Iowa, but they spend a lot of time with us. Since my parents are divorced, it's especially nice to have my grandparents around.

Reaching light switches on the wall is another real pain, so we have special pulls attached to all of ours. And we have stools all over the

house so I can do things that lots of people take for granted—like getting things out of the refrigerator when they're on a high shelf, or brushing my teeth in a comfortable position. Houses are definitely designed for tall people. Come to think of it, most of the outside world is designed for tall people. Whenever I go to the arcade at the mall, I have to get a small stool to stand on. I sing in the choir on Sundays and stand on a stool so I can be the same height as everyone else. Whenever I go to the movies, I sit in the front row to get the best view. I like to see the whole screen, right down to the bottom. Drinking fountains can be a problem. I usually pull myself up with my arms. Sometimes, it's hard for me to open doors because they're too heavy. One thing I'm really good at, though, is crawling behind the sofa if Mommy's lost something back there.

I'm a member of the Little People's Society of America. We have a few parties during the year and I get to meet other short-statured people. Mommy says it's been especially helpful for her to talk to the teenagers so she can know what to expect down the road. Most of the older kids have had an operation to fix their legs and feel that it's been a big help.

At home we always read the LPA newsletter, which helps everyone learn about what's going on. We also learned a lot from a book called *Thinking Big* by Susan Kuklin, which is about an eight-year-old girl who's a dwarf. Her name is Jaime, and her life is a lot like mine. But we're different in many ways. She has to wear protective knee pads when she plays sports because she has weak joints. She also has a hard time regulating her body temperature. In the winter she doesn't feel the cold the way average-sized people do, and in the summer she feels really warm. She's what is known as an achondroplastic dwarf, which is the most common variety—about eighty percent of dwarfs are in this group. These dwarfs often have lots of problems with their bones and with their circulation. They also have respiratory problems, which means it's hard for them to

breathe. Some dwarfs have trouble using their fingers because their hands aren't formed the same as everyone else's. They look as if their palms are little and their fingers are big. My kind of dwarfism was caused by a gene mutation and isn't as bad. Most people don't realize that there are at least 150 kinds of dwarfism. There are 30,000 dwarfs in the United States. I know I'm better off than most because I have fewer medical problems. Mommy says I'm also better off because I have a sunny disposition.

Even though most people do know something about dwarfs, they still stare whenever I go to the beach. I can see them looking at me.

When they ask me my age, they usually don't believe me, even if my brother's with me and says I'm telling the truth.

I love palling around with my brother Michael. He's been a big help. I don't get too involved in sports—a little kickball and tag is about all I do. What I like best is riding my bike with Michael. My being a dwarf has been tough on him because I get more attention. Sometimes it's tougher on him than on me.

I guess the hardest part about being a short-statured person is that most people don't know much about us. They've read "Snow White and the Seven Dwarfs" and in that story the dwarfs are treated like little simpletons. That's not how we are. Our brains are fine!

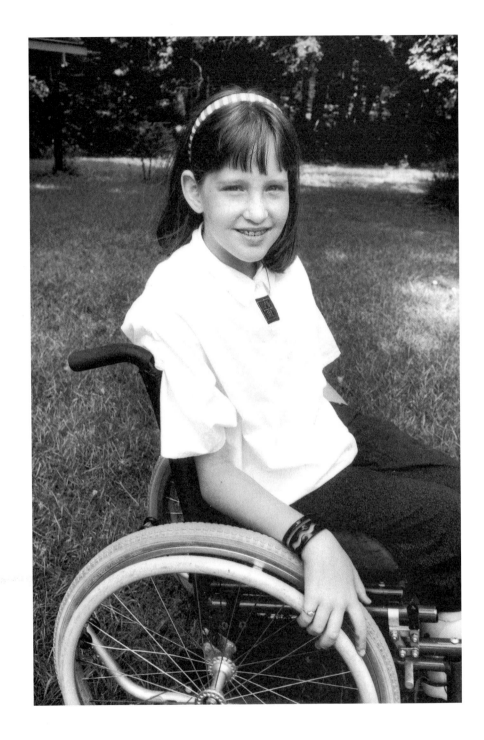

Katherine Lowe

AGE ELEVEN

I DON'T REMEMBER MUCH about the accident, since I was only four years old when it happened. My mom and dad and my two brothers, my sister, and I had been visiting our house on Dog Island, which is not far from Tallahassee, Florida, for the weekend and we were on our way home in my father's airplane. It was raining hard—so hard that my mother suggested we wait until the next morning to leave. But school was starting the next day, so we decided to take off anyway.

Dog Island is really small—its landing strip is just grass. We tried to take off against the wind but with no luck. Then my father turned around to take off with the wind. We got off the ground, but my dad lifted the wheels too soon and we went down into a ditch.

After it happened, I can remember hearing my mother calling out to me, and there was a terrible smell of gas because the tank had been punctured. My brother Tarver wasn't hurt, so he could climb out a window to get help. Luckily, there were people nearby who had seen the crash, and there was a doctor on the island who gave us emergency treatment. Soon helicopters arrived to take us to Tallahassee Memorial Hospital.

Tarver and my sister Sarah were lucky. They were barely hurt. The rest of us weren't as lucky. My dad hit the steering stick and died, and my mom barely made it. She broke about every bone you can imagine, and she was in a coma for a while. When the plane crashed, Chesley went straight forward and broke his back. I went forward, too, but I twisted to the left and that stretched my spinal column, causing swelling and damage to the nerves. Chesley's back got better, but mine never did.

I can't remember how long I stayed in Tallahassee, but altogether I was in various hospitals for more than five months. I was sent to Piedmont Hospital in Atlanta, Georgia, to have surgery on my back and then I went to Shepherd's Spinal Center, which is connected to Piedmont, for rehabilitation.

The people at Shepherd's were very nice, but I was scared anyway. I hadn't seen my mom in two months, and when she finally came to visit me, I didn't recognize her. She had to have plastic surgery because her face had hit the control panel, and she looked very different. She sometimes stayed with me and I slept on a cot on the other side of my hospital room when she came to see me. I stayed at Shepherd's for five months, from October until the beginning of March. During this time my brothers and sister visited me at least once a week. I went home for Christmas on a five-day pass but it was a very sad time for all of us because we missed Dad so much. Everyone tried to be strong for everyone else, but inside we felt terrible. Mom was still in a brace that went from her hips up to under her arms, and she was in a lot of pain. But she still tried to make Christmas as magical as it had always been.

When I came home for good, even though I was glad to be out of the hospital and back with my family, it was a mixed bag. I had felt abandoned by my mom when I was in the hospital and now I felt abandoned by my dad. And, on top of all that, I was strapped into a wheelchair. I couldn't walk!

At first, I had a lot of trouble getting used to not being able to walk. I would sit in the wheelchair all day long. Finally, the doctors attached a buzzer to my chair that went off every thirty minutes. Every time I heard the buzzer, I'd have to push myself up from the chair for sixty seconds. These are called weight shifts, and they prevent you from getting pressure sores on your bottom. I had to do this for about a year and a half! I don't do it anymore, because I don't often stay in one place for long.

I started using a standing board when I was in second grade. I stand

up on it and it holds me upright when I'm in class. It even has a desktop attached to it so that I can take notes. The standing board and my walker keep me up and about so that my leg muscles don't stiffen. If the muscles in the front of my legs stiffen up too much, my hips go out of joint. I had to have surgery on my hips once, because my muscles tightened up too much.

I also have a walker, which I mainly use around the house. I can't use it for long trips since it takes a lot of energy for me to hold myself upright and move around. My ankles are very weak, which makes it hard for me to stand up, even if I'm wearing braces on my legs.

I'm now a sixth grader at Stratford Academy in Macon, Georgia. I'm the only kid in my school who is in a wheelchair, but it doesn't bother me. Besides a flat tire or a broken spoke once in a while, the only time it's a problem is when I have to get to classes on the lower level. Since I can't use stairs with my wheelchair, I have to go all the way around the other side of the school in order to avoid them.

I'm leading as normal a childhood as possible. I play tennis. I swim. I can do anything if I put my mind to it, including keeping up with my older brothers and sister. I can even do some things that they can't. I probably spend more time with Sarah than with my brothers—she's more like a best friend than an older sister. She's always doing little things for me, like helping me experiment with different hairstyles—silly things, but fun. Chesley and Tarver are typical big brothers; sometimes they're OK but when they're fixing to go, they can be a big pain. Whenever I get really mad at them, or their friends, I just run over their toes with my wheelchair. That usually keeps them from being mean to me for a while.

Swimming is one of my favorite activities. I take lessons three times a week for two hours. I have to wear socks with heavy soles in the

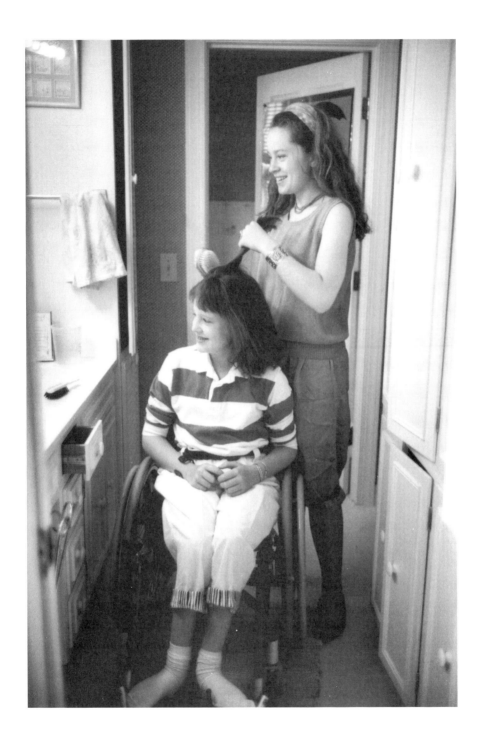

pool since I have no feeling in my legs. If I scrape my feet on the bottom, I can't feel any pain. Besides, if I scrape my feet it takes twice as long for me to heal, since my circulation isn't very good.

When I was six, I learned how to sit-ski. One day my mom said to me, "Hey, why don't we go skiing?" I said, "I can't ski." Then she told me that there are special skiing programs in Vail, Colorado. As it turned out, my school's ski group had already booked space at a resort in Vail that had sit-skiing, so off we went! We've been going ever since, and it's lots of fun.

When I ski, I sit on a thing that looks like a toboggan, with my legs straight out in front of me. There are two runners under the sled which are similar to the edges of a ski. First, I strap myself in with what looks like a seat belt, and then I zip myself into a waterproof cover. I have two miniature ski poles which are about six inches long and look like ice picks sticking through round metal disks.

Sometimes the other skiers are interested in my sit-ski and how it works. Lots of times they don't even realize I have a disability—they just think I'm going sledding. If they ask me why I'm using it, I explain to them that it's because I can't use my legs. They usually want to know how it works, and they love it if I let them hold one of my little poles.

My instructor's name is Ruth Flood, and she's wonderful. As soon as I'm ready to roll, she pulls me over to the chair lift and then she and a "lifter" ask the lift operator to please slow down the chair lift so they can put me on. There's a hook on the back of my sit-ski that fits over the back of the lift chair and the whole procedure is quite easy. After I'm strapped on, Ruth sits down beside me. When we get to the top of the mountain, she unhooks my sit-ski and makes sure I'm correctly positioned to go down the mountain. When she

says, "Tether is on," it means I can push off with my picks. I'm tethered with what looks like an orange nylon climbing harness, which is about twelve feet long. Ruth wraps it around her hand a few times so that she's about nine feet behind me, but as we pick up speed she extends the tether to the full twelve feet.

As we're zooming down, if I'm not leaning far enough to the right or left when making my turns, Ruth will say, "Commit right" or "Commit left," which means I have to lean over even farther. A "wipe out" is if I lean over too far and the sled tips over sideways. When I first started on the sit-ski, they actually taught me how to wipe out in case the instructor lost the tether. If that happened, I would be like a wild ski coming down the mountain, so I had to learn how to stop before picking up too much speed. At Vail, anyone who sit-skis is required to be tethered.

I love skiing with Ruth. She's a great skier and a great teacher. I think it's because she loves what she's doing so much. She's been working in the Vail program for the physically challenged for four years, and besides working with paraplegics like me, she teaches amputees as well as skiers who are deaf or blind or have cerebral palsy. She also works with children who have developmental disabilities like Down's syndrome, or with learning problems like Attention Deficit Disorder.

Whenever Ruth gets a student with a disability she hasn't worked with, she does a lot of research on her own so she'll have a better understanding of who she's working with and how she can be the most helpful. She thinks of sports like skiing and fishing as environmental therapy, and her goal is to become the "Dr. Ruth" of this kind of occupational therapy for kids like me. She lives in a condominium that is used by blind and deaf students, so she's learning sign language which she uses on the slopes. I've even learned to sign a little myself, because when we stop for lunch she teaches me some of what she's learned. But what she's taught me the most is how much difference a person like herself can make to people like me. She's made me feel I can do about anything I put my mind to doing. She knows how to push me to the limits without making me feel pressured or taking the fun out of what I'm doing.

This year at Vail, Ruth and I decided I should try a monoski. There's a bucket seat which sits on a spring shock which is attached to a single ski. I'm secured with four straps and I sit with my legs out in front of me. My poles are called outriggers and they clamp on to my forearms. Each pole has what looks like the tip of a ski at the bottom end. To tell you the truth, I wasn't all that convinced I was ready to do this because I've gotten so comfortable with the sit-ski, and besides, when you're sitting on the ground you can't fall over. But good old Dr. Ruth said I should give it a try, and promised me that once I got used to it I would love it. She also bribed me by reminding me I'd stay warmer, and drier, because I wouldn't have so much snow flying in my face.

We started by practicing indoors at the Children's Ski Center. I needed to work on my balance so I would feel confident that the chair wouldn't tip over. Ruth stood behind me and showed me how to initiate a turn using an outrigger. She told me to lean forward and pretend I was turning a door handle away from my body. If I turn with my right outrigger, I'll turn to the right, and with my left, to the left. It felt a little more scary than a sit-ski because I really could tip over. But Ruth promised me that even when we went down the mountain she would be right behind me, not tethered, but holding on to the chair, and that she wouldn't let me tip over. So that helped a lot because she's *never* broken a promise. She says that after I learn and build up my confidence, even if I do start tipping I'll be able to recover my balance. Besides, she says that falling over isn't all that terrible. All skiers fall. You just have to know how to get up—and she'll be teaching me that before I know it.

My mom's so excited about my learning the monoski she can hardly stand it. I'll be able to get on and off the lifts myself, and, after I master it, I won't even need an instructor. Mommy says she'll probably buy me my own monoski after I've got the hang of it because then we can go anywhere in the country that has snow!

In the summertime, we sometimes go to Cape Cod, Massachusetts. My mother has been spending summers there since she was a little girl. I have friends who are great about helping me get down to the ocean in my wheelchair. They also got me interested in playing tennis. I took lessons for a while and now I bring my racquet with me every summer.

My mom travels with us a lot. Mainly we drive places, but we do fly sometimes. Once we went to the Bahamas, and we had to take a small plane to get there. It was a Bonanza, the same kind we were flying in when we crashed. We were all a little nervous, but it was important for us to fly in a small plane again and see that it's usually perfectly safe.

I'm very lucky that I still have such a wonderful mom. She's had to be very strong to raise four kids on her own, especially with me to take care of. I try to make things as easy as possible, but there are some things I can't do by myself yet—as much as I would like to.

The main thing I need help with is emptying my bladder. Whenever I feel I need to go, my mother helps me insert a catheter, which is like a valve. We have to do this several times a day. First, we put a medicine called Betadine, which is like iodine, on the catheter, because if there are germs on it, I get a bladder infection which hurts. Otherwise, the catheter is easy to use. I tilt my body up while sitting in a chair, and we put it in. It doesn't hurt at all. This summer I'm going to the New England Medical Center to practice inserting the catheter myself. It's more complicated when you have to do it to yourself, because you can't see what you're doing down there. I will need to use a mirror.

At lunchtime, my mother has to come to school to catheterize me. We go to the women's bathroom, which is more private. Sometimes my friends ask me why I'm always disappearing into the teachers' bathroom. I'm not ashamed to tell them the truth, but it's embarrassing to be put on the spot that way. It's even more embarrassing when I leak. I wear special bladder control pads all the time. They're great because nobody can tell that I'm wearing them and they save the day in case I have an accident. Luckily, I don't leak that often and it's usually when I'm asleep at night.

In a few years, I may be able to have an operation that will make going to the bathroom much easier. They implant a valve in your bladder that you can open and close by remote control. I could just push a button when I need to go, and I wouldn't have to use a catheter at all. I can't wait until I stop growing so I can have the surgery. I won't have to impose on my mother all the time, and I won't get bladder infections anymore.

The catheter and the bladder infections are pretty much the worst part of having a disability, though I really hate going to public places and having other children stop and stare at me. I wish people wouldn't say, "Oh, that poor kid, she's in a wheelchair," because losing my dad was much harder for me than losing the use of my legs. He was an ear, nose, and throat surgeon and an experienced pilot. It was from him that I learned to discipline myself. He always said, "If you carry out what you believe in, you'll always reach your goal."

Some Sundays after church, my mom takes me to visit my father's grave. I don't exactly feel on top of the world when we go there, but I know that I'm doing something good by remembering him— not that I'd ever forget! My mother has never remarried, and I have to admit that I'm glad that she hasn't. I'd like having my regular old dad back. It may sound crazy, but I would feel uncomfortable having a stranger walk into the house at the end of the day. As it is, we're a large family and everybody is very supportive and close.

I have a lot of faith that I'll be able to walk again. When I broke my back, a lot of nerves were damaged, but my spinal cord wasn't severed. My mom has read lots of articles about operations doctors are working on that could help people with injuries like mine to walk again. This is way in the future, and I believe it will happen.

If someone asked me to describe myself, I would say I'm a person who can't walk but who can do everything else. That may sound conceited, but I don't really care what other people think. People who put me down are just putting themselves down, and I'm not going to let that stop me.

Kevin Watson

IT WASN'T UNTIL I was a year old that my mother realized that something was wrong with me. I couldn't sit up straight and I couldn't stand. I was still crawling on the floor and pulling myself along with my hands.

My mother spoke to my pediatrician and he referred her to another doctor. The other doctor couldn't see me for six months because he had so many other appointments. But finally we went, and he told my parents that he thought I had cerebral palsy. He wasn't sure because he was an orthopedic doctor, so my mom went to United Cerebral Palsy, which is an organization that specializes in the care of kids with cerebral palsy. The doctors did a lot of tests on me—measuring some of my movements and observing me—and said I did have CP. By then I was two and a half. And by then I had lost a lot of valuable time.

At this stage, a lot of different people evaluated me in different areas. They tested my cognitive development, which means was I functioning on a two-year-old level—was my vocabulary up to snuff for a two-year-old? They tested my fine motor skills, my ability to hold a pencil and draw, or my ability to hold a wooden block and put it in a similarly shaped hole—little things that people take for granted every day. They tested my major motor skills by having me throw a ball, or walk, or stand on one foot. They played games with me to see what I could and couldn't do. I don't remember any of this but my parents have told me about it so often I know all the details by heart.

I was classified as a spastic quadriplegic, which means I had some spasticity in my legs and arms. Spasticity is like stiffness, so when I moved my arms and legs they jerked instead of moving in a fluid way. And when I tried to walk, my legs would cross so I could only take about four steps before losing my balance and falling down. Mentally, I was fine.

I was taken into the Cerebral Palsy Program and the main purpose of this program was to make me independent. They taught me how to get in and out of my clothing. They even toilet trained me, which wasn't so easy. Imagine how difficult it was for me to learn how to urinate when it was very hard to keep my balance while standing up. I was in the program for about three hours a day at first, and as I got older it was like a regular school from nine to three. I stayed in the program until I was about six years old.

Besides helping me, the people at the Cerebral Palsy Program really helped my parents. There's a branch near where we live and my mom and dad got very involved with the parents' support group. One of the problems that parents of kids with disabilities have is finding baby-sitters to take care of their kids so they can go out once in a while for dinner or a movie. All the parents in the support group took turns baby-sitting for each other. Since all the kids had

CP, all the parents knew exactly what to do. My mom and dad used to sit for one particular boy who was in a wheelchair all the time. He couldn't eat by himself and he had to be fed. The muscles in his throat prevented him from swallowing easily and his speech was slurred. A lot of kids with CP have trouble talking. There's nothing wrong with their brains, but their muscles are affected in a way that makes it hard for them to get the words out. I feel sorry for them because I think they have a hard life not being able to communicate with other people. Now that I'm older I don't need a baby-sitter anymore, but when I was younger this parents' group saved the day. My mom and dad needed some time away from me, and I needed time away from them.

When I was five and a half, I had a major five-hour operation. Dr. Leon Root, who is an orthopedic surgeon at the Hospital for Special Surgery in New York City, released my thigh muscles, cut the Achilles tendons in both my legs, and he lengthened some muscles on the insides of my feet while shortening some others on the outside. I had to wear a body cast from the waist down—it's called a spica—and I had to wear it for six weeks. It was summer and boy was it hot. My parents picked me up by holding the back of my head with one hand and the bar on my spica cast with the other hand. The bar was inserted into the plaster cast, horizontally between my two legs. They gave me an appliance with little wheels on it—it looked like a scooter without an upright handle—and if someone placed me on top of it, tummy down, I could get around like a human skateboard. Before the operation, my feet were such a big problem that I couldn't walk, but afterwards I was able to learn how with the help of a therapist.

Several months after the operation I went back to school, and I was able to graduate from the program six months later, in June. By then, I was out of the cast and able to walk across the floor to get my certificate. My parents said there wasn't a dry eye in the house. My mother cried the hardest.

Even though the operation had been a big success and I could finally walk, I still couldn't go up and down stairs. So now my parents had to find me a regular school with everything on one level. We found the school, but they required me to use a wheelchair because I was still somewhat wobbly. They were nervous that some of the other children might hurt me, accidentally, while they were running through the halls.

I was the only student with a physical challenge who was main-streamed into this school. When I first started, there were some kids who kept on bugging me and made fun of the way I walked, but after a while they got used to me. Even though Dr. Root encouraged me to use crutches or a walker for a while to improve my gait, I didn't want to because I was warned I'd get dependent on them.

I also had to have an aide at first, but after six months I was able to convince everyone that I didn't need one. I ditched the wheelchair too. My parents went to the principal and told him I should be treated like the other kids, and that if I got a few bruises it was no big deal. They said they wouldn't hold the school responsible.

My second operation was to fix my knees, which were very stiff and didn't bend much. This operation was easier. A physical therapist came to the house and worked with me for about half an hour every day during the summer. By the time September rolled around, I was able to go back to school and be in the fourth grade. I'm in the fifth grade now.

I probably won't have any more operations, but I will keep working with my physical therapist three days a week. Her name is Debbie

Scalise and she comes to my school to work with me. She works with me for about half an hour or forty-five minutes each time. We try to build up my strength so I won't get so tired when I walk.

I can walk about four or five blocks on my own without getting too tired, but if it's more than that I often get a wheelchair. It's always a hard decision for me, though, because there are lots of times when I know it's easier, and faster, for all of us if I use a wheelchair. On the other hand, I don't like to be thought of as handicapped, and if you're in a wheelchair, that's how people are going to think of you. The last time we went to Disneyland, I managed to get around on my own. I got tired but I kept on going, and it made me feel good about myself. I try to act like other kids and live a normal life. I can't do sports, but otherwise I get around fine.

My therapist is trying to get me some new orthotics for my feet, which are starting to turn out. They look like small plastic braces which have been molded to my feet and ankles. I have a big plastic bag under my bed which is full of the pairs I've grown out of or that aren't comfortable. It's a bit of trial and error with orthotics. You just have to keep trying different ones until you get a good fit. I have to wear regular shoes, which are usually sneakers, that are big enough to fit over the orthotics. But it's worth the discomfort because with them I can get around on my own two feet. I used to have to go up and down steps on my butt or on my stomach, but with my orthotics I can climb stairs by holding on to the railing.

Besides having trouble walking, I also have some difficulty with what are called my fine motor skills. I write more slowly than the other kids so I have trouble finishing tests in the same amount of time as my classmates. We have a resource room in our school where I can receive some special attention. I don't seem to have any real learning disabilities but I do need some extra help with some of my subjects, especially spelling. My favorite subject is creative writing. Last year one of my teachers recommended me for the "Yes, I Can" program and one of the stories I wrote was chosen to receive an award. It was selected from over 1,500 submissions.

I used to go to a special camp in the summer called LEAP, which was run by the Easter Seal Society. It was the only camp we could find which would not only take kids with a handicap but also let their siblings come too. My sister Samantha and I both went for two years. I wish I could go away every summer, but there are a limited number of kids who can go, so I had to give other kids the chance to experience it. As a result of my going to the summer camp, the Easter Seal people wanted me to be on their nationally televised telethon. We raised over a million dollars. The New York Easter Seal Society helps kids with all kinds of disabilities. Besides making arrangements for kids to go to their camp, they also arrange for financial aid for some families.

The Cerebral Palsy Foundation also has a summer camp, but most of the kids who go are much worse off than I am and that tends to make me depressed. I'm much happier when I'm playing with kids who don't have any disabilities. I know I make life harder on myself that way. I can't always keep up with them, but it's a price I'm willing to pay for the chance to at least try.

My mom wants me to be as independent as possible in case anything ever happens to her. She wants me to learn how to compensate now, even though at times it may be rough for me. I think she's right, because when I get older I'm going to have to get a good job and be on my own. My parents can't take care of me forever.

I think I'm very lucky that *everyone* has pushed me toward independence—my parents, my doctor, my teachers, and my therapist. But all the pushing in the world would not have helped if it wasn't what *I* wanted.

Sarah Reinertsen

AGE FOURTEEN

I WAS BORN WITH a birth defect called proximal focal femoral deficiency—or, more simply put, an underdeveloped thigh. What happened is that even before I was born, I didn't have enough tissue in my left leg to stimulate growth. As I started to grow, my left femur—or thighbone—only grew partially, so my knee was right up against my hip, with my foot hanging parallel to my right knee. The doctors aren't sure why this happened. My mom says she was sick with a virus during her pregnancy and she thinks my disability may have been caused by the medication she was given.

I have had a prosthesis, or artificial limb, since I was eleven months old. Walking was natural for me—they put on my prosthesis and off I went. The problem was, my left knee bent up near my hip, so I had to swing my other leg all the way around every time I took a step. When I was seven, I had several operations to amputate my left foot and fuse my knee, so that I had a stump. I decided on the surgery because it made it possible for me to be fitted with an artificial leg that can bend where it's supposed to.

After the operation, I had to spend a month at the Rusk Institute in New York City, a rehabilitation center, learning to walk with my new leg. Rusk wasn't dreary like most hospitals; the mood was much lighter. The other patients and I would meet with our therapists in the morning and then we'd paint and draw and play games for the rest of the day. It was more like summer camp than a hospital situation.

The first prosthesis I got had a knee joint with a hinge on either side—kind of like door hinges. My parents and I were unaware of the new technologies available, so we ended up paying a big price for an artificial leg that was identical to the ones being made in the 1940s. That's what was given to us, so that's what we thought was the best. And if that wasn't bad enough, our original insurance plan only covered the cost of one prosthesis which, of course, was my first one—the one I got when I was eleven months old—which cost $500. Now they cost thousands and each time I have to get one repaired we're fighting the insurance company. The last time I got it repaired, the bill was $1,500.

The prosthesis I have now is much more advanced, with top-of-the-line components such as a Flex-Foot, a suction socket, and a hydraulic knee. I've been growing very quickly for the past couple of years, and my prosthetist, Michael Joyce, was pulling his hair out—each leg costs around $10,000! Fortunately we have a new system where, instead of making an entire leg, Michael makes a new socket and lengthens the leg a bit. It's much cheaper, and it only takes about a day to make an adjustment, so we're all happy.

Whenever I need an adjustment, Michael first takes a plaster cast of my residual limb, or stump, and then fills the mold with plaster,

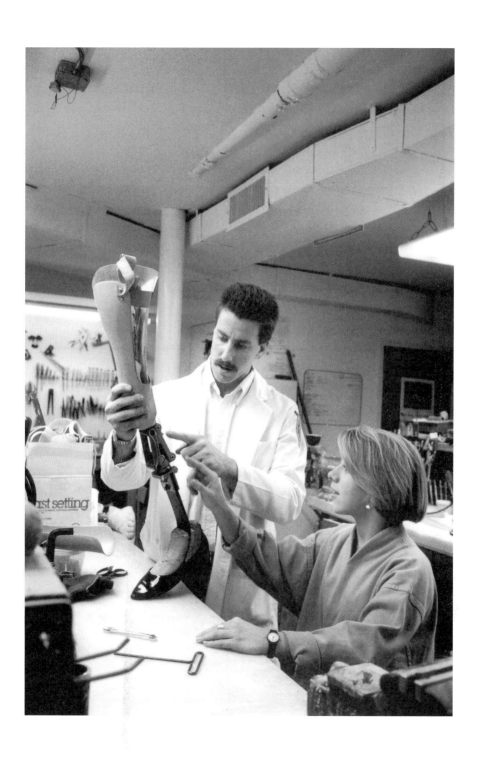

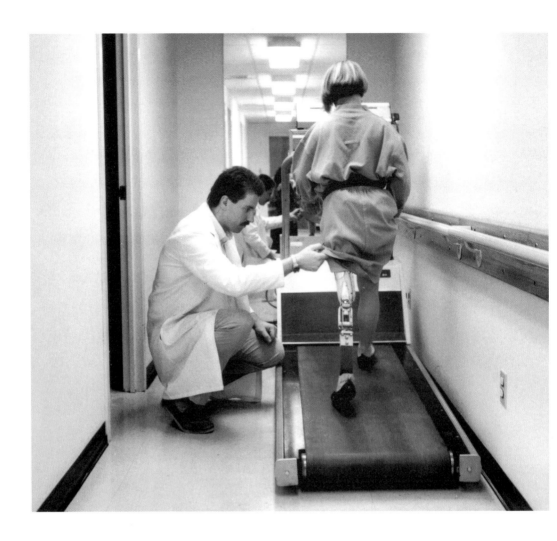

so that he ends up with an exact model. The socket is molded to fit over the limb perfectly, and then the leg is built around the socket. An artificial leg is made of a series of layers. First, there's a silicone liner that I wear over my stump. The liner works like a Chinese finger trap—it rolls onto my residual limb very easily, but suction prevents it from sliding off. The liner attaches to the leg with Velcro and keeps it from falling off. The next layer is a socket of clear plastic held in a rigid frame made of graphite. This protects the limb and is flexible enough to change shape as I walk or sit down, which makes it much more comfortable.

My hydraulic knee is made of titanium, which doesn't rust and is three times stronger than steel. My old knee used to rust if I got it wet. We had a family joke that I could never be a burglar because they'd hear me coming a mile away. My friends wrote a poem about me which went like this:

> Hi, my name is Sarah
> and you'll find me in a crowd
> 'cause wherever I walk
> my leg is too loud.

Now, there's a cylinder inside my knee which is filled with oil. My prosthetist adjusts the way the oil flows through the cylinder so that the faster I walk, the more resistance it provides—just like the muscles in a real knee—which allows me to move more naturally. Learning to walk on it was a frustrating experience at first, since I felt like I had to relearn all the basics of walking, but it's much more sophisticated than any other prosthesis I've had.

It's really important to check regularly to make sure that a leg fits properly. If it doesn't, your spinal alignment is thrown off, because you're not walking evenly. Also, a poorly fitting prosthesis can rub against the stump and be really painful. Of course, how often you go to the prosthetist depends on how active you are. A less active person wouldn't have to go that often. When you're younger, you're much harder on your legs, especially if you're a runner, like me.

My parents and younger brother Peter are all runners, and they have always encouraged me to stay very active. When I was younger, my parents sent me to a regular nursery school, to swimming lessons and camp—everything other kids did. Every summer, we go hiking and camping together in upstate New York. I think my family's encouragement has a lot to do with the fact that I have such a positive attitude. They never sat me in front of the TV or stopped me from doing anything I wanted to try. They gave me a normal childhood.

I became interested in competitive running three years ago, when I was eleven. Before that, I really didn't know there were other kids around who were like me. Even when I was at Rusk, there was very little talk about physically challenged kids getting involved in competitive athletics. Meeting Paddy Rossbach changed everything. My parents are both teachers, and they work together at a summer camp. One of the counselors remembered the way I ran around the camp when I was little, and he put my parents in touch with Paddy, who was starting a program for amputees. She's an amputee as well as a really good athlete—she holds the women's world record for an amputee running a marathon. A marathon is 26.2 miles long.

Paddy runs a program at the Hospital for Special Surgery called ASPIRE, which stands for Adolescent Sarcoma Patients' Intense Rehabilitation with Exercise. I became involved in the program, and Paddy entered me in my first competition, the New York State Games for the Physically Challenged. I participated in two track events and two swimming events and came home with four gold medals. A year later, in 1988, I set world records in the 100-, 200-, and 400-meter races at the Canadian National Championships in Calgary. The competitive spirit in me rose out of that. That's when I started to set a lot of goals for myself. I never cover my leg when I compete because when my opponents see my Flex-Foot it psyches them out.

Besides doing a lot of aerobic exercise, a part of being in the ASPIRE program involves taking tests. The average amputee uses around two to three times more energy to walk or run than a person who isn't physically challenged. Paddy is working with the Hospital for Special Surgery to train amputees the same way all athletes train—strengthening their heart and lungs, and making them more efficient so that they use less energy. Every six months I take a test that measures my oxygen intake. I put on a mask with a mouthpiece that is connected to a big bag I wear on my back. There are lights all around the testing room flashing at different speeds. I walk at the

speed the lights flash, and as I breathe, the machine collects the gases I exhale and measures my heart rate, which Ann Barr, my physical therapist, writes down on my chart. In the end, the doctor can tell how much oxygen I used during the exercise. I'm in pretty good shape now, so I only use about one and a half times as much oxygen as able-bodied people.

Some of the tests they give at ASPIRE try to judge the way you feel about yourself. Every time I get my oxygen intake measured, I answer a lot of questions. They are all multiple-choice, and ask you things like how you feel about your body. They kind of let you know where you stand. I don't mind the tests, but it's sort of weird to think you've become a statistic. There are so many mixed emotions involved in being a person with a disability that it's hard to express your feelings by filling in bubbles with a number 2 pencil.

Some of my mixed emotions have to do with straightforward physical things. Standing on my feet for a long time can be painful, and stairs are pretty annoying, too. I have to take one step up with my right leg, bring my prosthesis up to the same level and then start all over again. I don't have enough hip motion to go quickly, so if I'm trying to rush to a class in school I usually have to take two steps at a time. Things aren't always easy for me, and there are times when I think, "Why me?" but I don't want anyone to pity me. I can carry things on my own, I can walk and run, and I can achieve a lot.

Sometimes I have dreams that I have two legs, but they're not necessarily more positive than the dreams where I have one. I don't miss walking on two legs because I never have. If I asked people to explain to me what it feels like to walk on two legs, they couldn't do it, because it's so natural for them. And it's natural for me to walk and run the way I do.

One experience that did discourage me a little was being on my school track team. I was the only girl on the team who didn't have two legs, so I was constantly struggling to keep up with most of the other girls. I knew that I couldn't be compared to them because running on two legs is so different from running on one leg, but I would still get frustrated when I would see that they could run a couple of laps ahead of me with so little effort. It was always in the back of my mind that if I had two legs I could do it, so I've decided to stick with competing against others who are in the same boat as I am.

I try to enter in as many competitions for people with disablities as possible. The only problem is, I'm too young to participate in most of the international competitions. I sent in my application to run in

the World Championships for the Disabled in Holland, but you have to be sixteen to participate in track-and-field events. I'm hoping to go to the 1992 Paralympics in Barcelona, since I should be old enough then to qualify. We're waiting to see if they'll allow female above-the-knee amputees to compete. In the meantime, this summer I'm going to France for the World Youth Games. Up until now, besides Canada, I've only competed in the United States.

It's interesting to compete in other countries because I think other cultures are less ignorant about people with disabilities. There is a type of prejudice in the United States against people who have handicaps. It was hardest when I was younger. In junior high and high school, kids are pretty mature; but on a younger level, if someone wants to hurt you, they pick on your obvious weakness, which in my case was my artificial leg. When I was younger, if the other children made fun of me in school—and they did—I didn't say anything to them. I felt sorry for *them* because I figured if that's the way their minds worked, *they* were handicapped—not me.

The other way that people show their ignorance is by staring. When I was young, it used to bother me, because I didn't realize that they didn't understand my disability. Kids would say to their parents, "Hey, Mom, look at that!" and the parent would say, "Shh, don't ask questions." It always made me angry, because I think it's important for everyone to know the full story. Unless people learn about disabilities early on, they won't really accept the physically challenged as normal people. Now, when I'm baby-sitting or in school or down at the beach, the responsibility falls on me to educate people. I think education is very important. If a kid comes up and asks me about my leg, I'll explain that I was born with one leg shorter than the other, so I have to wear an artificial one in order to walk. Sometimes it's hard to explain—you just have to make it up as you go along.

Lately, someone I've been working with at the gym has arranged

for me to go to some schools and give talks about being physically challenged, about dealing with it, and about doing sports. Todd Schaffhauser and Dennis Oehler, who are both champion athletes and amputees, do it too. It's really great. You talk, and maybe show videotapes, and demonstrate running. The kids are very interested and ask a lot of questions. Most often, they ask me whether I swim, sleep, and shower with my artificial leg. The answer to all three questions is no. Sometimes it's hard to make people understand, but I think a program like this is important. If I can do anything to change people's attitudes about the physically challenged, that's more rewarding to me than winning medals.

I know it sounds strange, but I'm glad I was born with my disability because I've had so many opportunities that I never would have had otherwise. When you have a physical disability, it strengthens you mentally. Being an amputee is the greatest thing that could have happened to me.

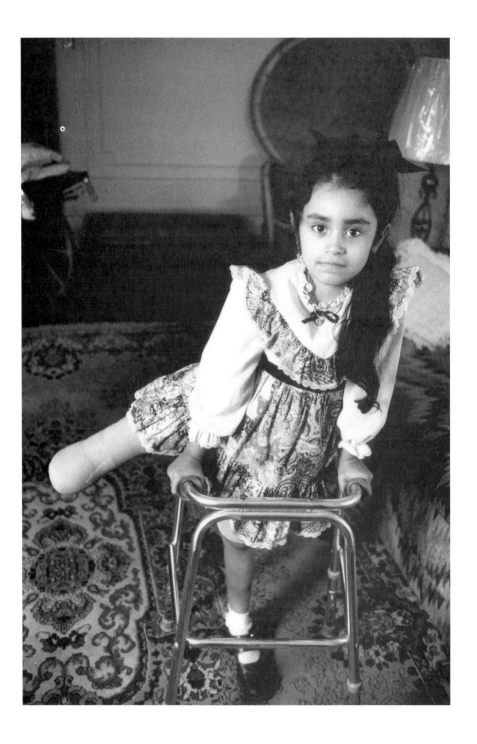

Krystle Bonet

I WAS BORN WITH one leg much shorter than the other. My mom has told me my short leg looked like a regular leg. It had a foot and a knee, but the part between the hip and the knee which is called the femur was very little—it was less than an inch long. When I was three months old, the doctors put me in a special harness to correct my hip which hadn't grown properly. I wore that for three months and then they made me another kind of brace that I wore until I was one.

On my first birthday, I was fitted with a leg so I could learn to walk. It's called a prosthesis, and mine was made out of plastic and plaster. It was painted to match the color of my other leg. That's the first thing I really remember. I wore that for five years and it was pretty good. Of course, I had to get a bigger one every time I grew out of the one I was using. The only trouble was that my "pretend leg" didn't bend at the knee, so I couldn't run as fast as my friends. Also, if my mom took me on a bus or a train my leg would stick out when

I sat down. The same thing happened when my mom took me to a movie. I couldn't go to the movies unless I sat in the front row so there would be room for my leg. I had problems in restaurants too, because I always had to have an empty chair in front of me to prop my leg on. At first, my school didn't want to keep me because they were worried I might fall and hurt myself.

I had my first surgery just after my fifth birthday. They grafted some bone from one place on my body in order to make a hip joint for me. This was the first time I stayed in a hospital overnight and I stayed for five days. My mommy went to the hospital with me and slept in my room. My parents are divorced and my dad only visited me once. He had a hard time accepting my leg problem from the beginning and so, in a way, it was easier for my mom and me when he left because he wasn't very supportive. He would never let me wear dresses because he was embarrassed. Sometimes he would pull on my shortened leg hoping to make it grow. My mother told him that he had to accept what had happened and let me grow up like a normal little girl. But he couldn't, so they divorced. It's better this way, but it does make me a little sad.

I don't remember much about being in the hospital except that the nurses were nice to me and I hated the IVs. They're the worst. When they took me to the operating room I went right to sleep. They fixed my hip so my leg dropped down an extra half inch. I was in a spinal cast for three months after the surgery and I had to stay at home—in bed and in a wheelchair that I could lie in. My mom is an office manager at a hospital—she had to stop working full-time in order to take care of me. My grandmother stayed with me on the days Mommy worked. That December I went to Radio City Music Hall in my wheelchair to see *Snow White*. That was a very special day.

Then, after three months in the spinal cast, I went back to the hospital to have the pins removed from my hip. They put me to sleep again and this time I stayed in for two days. The doctors arranged for physical therapists—Kevin Loughlin and Cathi Wagner—to work with me twice a week. They put me in the swimming pool to do exercises and I loved it. It was the best. Then I started doing stretching exercises out of the pool, on the mats.

This past year the doctors did another operation, a knee fusion—and they cut off my foot. When Mommy told me what they were going to do, I cried and cried. I kept asking, "Why me, Mommy? Why me?" Mommy told me that after the operation the doctors would fit me with a prosthesis with a bending knee, and I'd be able to get around a lot more easily—that I could ride a bike and go roller-skating and do all the things I love doing. Mommy cried too, but she tried to be strong for me. I want to be a bone doctor when I grow up, and my leg doctor told me I'd be an even better doctor after my operation because I'd be such a good example for my patients.

This last operation was the worst, not because of the pain, but because they took part of me away. It's weird because even though I can see my foot is gone, it feels like it's still there. I asked my surgeon, Dr. Bohne, what they were going to do with my foot after they cut it off, and he told me they were going to take it to the laboratory to run some tests on it and then they would bury it. I wanted to keep it in a little jar, but they wouldn't let me.

After my operation, when they showed me my leg without the foot, I cried and cried. A doctor at the hospital came to see me twice a week. She told me she was a psychiatrist and she tried to help me but she didn't really. Mommy, my uncle Willie, and my grandmother helped me the most because they kept telling me things would be better. And they didn't ask me a lot of questions like the pyschiatrist did.

I still cry when people remind me of what I went through. I don't like to talk about my operation or think about it if I don't have to.

Sometimes people stare at me when I go out, and they ask my mom if I was in an accident. When she tells them I was born this way, they have a harder time accepting it. Some of the kids at school called me "robot leg." I told my mom I felt sorrier for them than for myself because they can't understand. Mommy took me to my classmates' houses and told their moms that she didn't want them calling me names. Now they treat me differently. They protect me and look after me. My mom says she feels gifted to have had me— gifted to have had a child with a healthy brain who can be independent—and she feels good about herself that she's been able to be both a mother and a father to me. I think we're lucky to have each other. Mommy has a new boyfriend now and I'm hoping they'll get married. His name is David Ruiz, and the reason I like him so much is because he accepts me just the way I am—being myself.

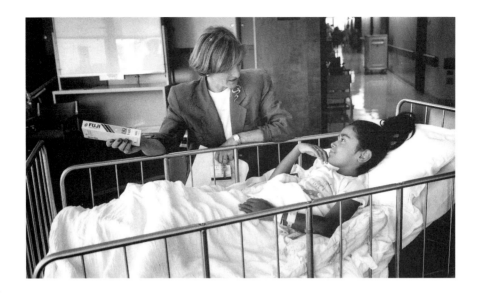

While I was still in the Hospital for Special Surgery, Paddy Rossbach came to visit me. She lost her leg when she was very young—she was hit by a car—and she's a great athlete. She brought me a video-tape about people like me who play sports and she promised me

I could be just like them. After I got out of the hospital, she took me to Mitchell Field where I got to meet three of her "prize runners"—Sarah Reinertsen, Dennis Oehler, and Todd Schaffhauser. All three of them hold world records. When Sarah was born, her leg was exactly like mine and she can do anything she wants to do. She makes me realize that anything is possible. She promised me that as soon as I got my new leg we would train together.

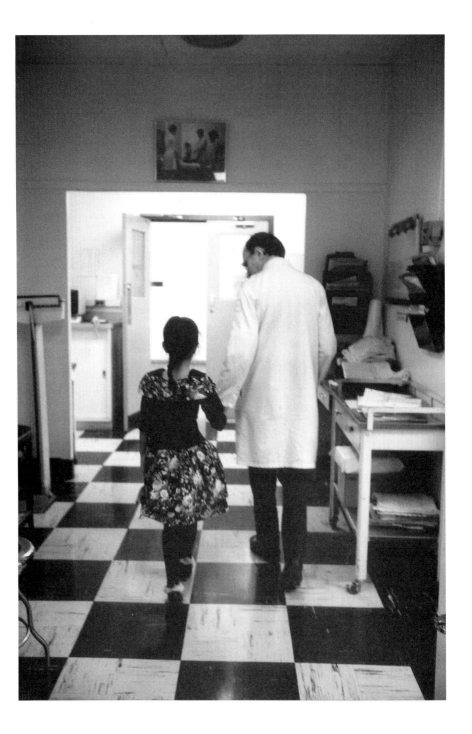

Well, a few weeks ago I did get my new leg! I'm still learning how to walk with it. I started off by using crutches but now I'm doing so well that I only need one crutch for balance. Before long, I won't be using anything. The last time I had a visit with Dr. Bohne, we walked up and down the hospital corridor together and he said I was doing great. He gave me a big hug and told me I'd soon be ready to start training with Sarah and the rest of the gang. I can't wait!

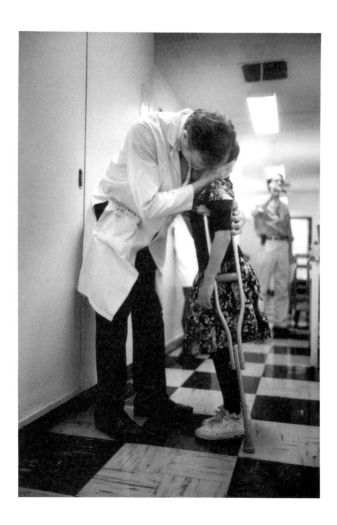

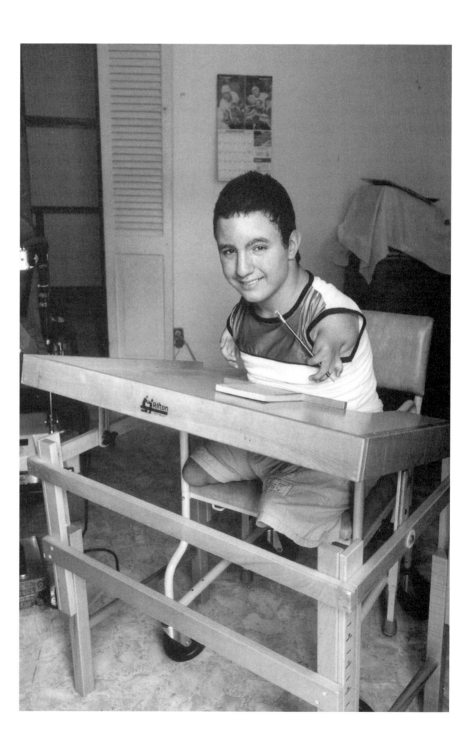

Joey Floccari

I WAS BORN WITH a disability called TAR, which stands for throm-bocytopenia absent radius. To be simpler about it, I have no arms or legs—my hands come out of my shoulders and I have stumps for legs. A lot of times when people see me, they ask my mother if she took thalidomide when she was pregnant. Thalidomide is a fer-tility drug women used to take that caused birth defects. My mother didn't take any kinds of drugs or medicine during her pregnancy. The condition I have is caused by something that went wrong in my genes.

I was only thirteen inches long when I was born. I had feet, but they were useless for walking because they were more like flippers than feet and couldn't support my weight. Also, I didn't have any ankles. When I was two, my doctors amputated my flipper feet so I could be fitted for artificial legs.

I can do a lot for myself, even without arms. I brush my teeth and

comb my hair without help, and I don't need any special utensils for eating. My mother puts a special plastic handle around cartons so that I can pour my own milk and juice, and I can get small things, like bread and a jar of jam, out of the refrigerator by myself. I spend a lot of time working on my computer, and I have an electric keyboard that I like to fiddle around with. It's all pretty easy if you're used to it. I even have a special system for picking things up with both hands. I lean down and put one hand on the floor, and then I stretch my other hand around to reach it. I can only do it when I'm lying on my side, so if I want to open a jar or something, I have to get down on the floor.

From the time I was born until I was three, I lived at a place called St. Mary's Hospital in Bayside, Long Island. At St. Mary's, all the kids had handicaps and, because I had never been in the outside world, I didn't realize that I was different from anybody else. The day I got out of the hospital to go live with my family, I suddenly found out that other kids weren't like me. It doesn't bother me now— if I'm at a store or something and people stare at me, I just turn the other way. But when I was little, it was a hard thing for me to discover.

While I was at St. Mary's, I learned how to crawl, and then eventually I learned to walk. I remember one day I was crawling on a mat, and

someone stood next to me and held my hand and told me to try and stand up. I just stood up and started walking on my stumps, and that was the beginning of things. After that, I kept practicing at the Rusk Institute where I went to get more physical therapy. I'm pretty good at it now.

A few years ago I got prosthetic legs—or "booties," which is what I call them. With the booties, I can walk around my whole school building once. I mainly wear them in school, because I get tired if I walk around too much. They work like boots and fit over my stumps. They're about two feet long and are made from leather— the same kind of leather they use for horse saddles. It's very soft but very tough. When I have them on, you can hear me coming from a mile away; that's how noisy they are. When they don't fit perfectly, they squeak a lot and recently I lost some weight, so they're louder than usual. I wear them five days a week when I'm at school, and I put them on if I have to go out somewhere on a weekend. They're a big help to me. Because I'm taller with my legs, I can reach a lot more things with them on. Also, I can get around a lot faster when I wear them. The only problem is that sometimes they rub and give me rashes. Then I have to go to a dermatologist. One time the doctor yelled at my mom as though it was her fault. It wasn't anyone's fault—not hers, not mine. It's just a fact of life when you have prostheses.

When I was six or seven years old, I tried out a couple of different kinds of prostheses. One pair made me about five feet tall. I couldn't walk on them at all, because I had to kick my foot every time I wanted to lift each leg and move it forward. When I was doing that, I fell. I didn't crack my head or anything; I just fell and someone caught me. But I couldn't wear those legs again. A while ago I brought them to school because someone wanted to see what they looked like. I just left them there and never use them.

I had another pair before that, but I kept falling until my grand-father built me crutches. I walked all over the house and I was losing weight and getting in shape, but then I fell against the wall and I was too scared to wear those anymore, either. Now that I'm bigger and stronger, I'm ready to try another pair. I think I'll have a much easier time walking on them. And I'm not so afraid of falling now. These prostheses will look more like real legs, with feet and every-thing, so I'll be able to wear shoes or sneakers.

When I'm not wearing my prosthetic legs, I use a wheelchair or I walk on my stumps. It's not easy to walk on my stumps in our house, since it has hard linoleum floors. It's all bone where my knees should be and it hurts to walk on it. Mom washes the floors every day without fail so I won't get any infections in case I have an open sore. In the summer, we spend every weekend at a house in Pennsylvania. The floors there are all covered with rugs, so it's a lot easier for me to get around.

Sometimes my family goes on trips to places other than Pennsylvania. We have a special van with a lift for my wheelchair so that I can travel with them without a problem. Our vacations take a lot of planning since we usually have to let the hotel or motel where we're staying know at least a month in advance that I'm physically chal-lenged. That way they have time to build a ramp, or do whatever they need to do to make the place wheelchair accessible. A lot of public places don't have doors wide enough to fit my chair, which can be a real problem—especially if it's the bathroom door!

I spend a lot of time sitting in a wheelchair. The chair I have now is electric. It runs off a battery, and I'm responsible for making sure the battery is charged up all the time. Every night I plug it in to recharge, and I have to replace it every year. If the battery goes dead, I can't move. This has only happened to me once, but it was horrible—I had to scream and shout for help. Everyone looked at me like I was crazy, but I was really scared. I won't let that happen again.

The chair was a gift from Variety, a charitable organization that has helped me a lot. Variety has a telethon every year to raise money for hospitals and for the homeless. They also give money to kids who need it. About four years ago, I saw the Variety telethon on television and thought it looked like fun. I asked my mother to look into it. I don't know exactly how she got in touch with them, but one of the people who work for them asked me if I would go on the telethon and I said yes. I sang on the show, and that year they made me their poster child. I've gone back every year since.

Singing is very important to me. I take lessons in Brooklyn, New York, where I live. Sometimes my teacher comes to my house, but mainly I go to his. He has a band that practices in his basement, so I go down there and sing with them. At home I practice singing the scales, which exercises my voice. The lessons don't just improve my voice—they also teach me how to breathe right and control my nerves. This is very helpful, since I get really nervous when I have to sing on TV.

Sometimes the telethon is filmed in a studio, and sometimes they have it at the Big Apple Circus, in front of an audience. It's scarier to perform in front of all the people at the circus, but I prefer it to the studio—I don't have to spend hours sitting in a dressing room getting made up, and there are more interesting things to look at.

My favorite kind of music is rock, but I like slow songs too. Last year I performed the song "Somewhere Out There," from the movie *An American Tail*. I sang that song for a holiday show at my school, and my parents sent a tape of me singing it to someone at Variety. They loved it, and they wanted me to sing it on the telethon, so I sang it. I hope I can perform at Variety every year.

We have a lot of plays and shows at my school—one year I played the Cowardly Lion in *The Wizard of Oz*. Something is always going on over there. I go to the Henry Viscardi School on Long Island, which was founded by a man named Henry Viscardi, who was born with no legs and was never allowed to go to school because of his disability. He is seventy-eight now, and he comes to visit almost every day.

Right now I'm in junior high. There are ten kids in my class, and between us, we've got just about every disability you can think of. There are kids with cerebral palsy, spina bifida, muscular dystrophy, and dwarfism. Going to this school has been easier for me than if I had gone to a regular school because we're all in the same boat. In fact, there are kids there who have worse problems than I have, like my friend who's paralyzed from the waist down. He has to breathe with a respirator, and it's hard for him to talk loudly. I think this school has helped me and the kids I know, so it should work for other people, too.

Even though everyone who goes there has a disability, Henry Viscardi is a lot like any other school—we have all the regular classes, and we have homework to do every night. I like science class because we get to do lots of experiments, but I think computer lab is my favorite. When I get older, I want to study computers at college and become a computer technician.

The main thing that's different about my school is that everything is adapted for people in wheelchairs. We even have a wheelchair maintenance class, which they teach us in woodshop. There are lots of ramps and railings at school, but they don't make things too easy

for us—if they did, we would get spoiled and we wouldn't be able to get along in the outside world.

Another thing that makes my school different is the amount of work we do to stay fit. There is a doctor, four nurses, and a whole bunch of therapists on call all the time. Every day I do occupational and physical therapy. The occupational therapist helps me get dressed and do everyday things, and the physical therapist helps me walk and exercise and all that. For example, since my right hand is weaker than my left, I do special exercises with my occupational therapist to make it stronger.

It's important for me to get all kinds of exercise because if I gained a few too many pounds, my stumps wouldn't be able to support my weight and I wouldn't be able to walk. This is a problem dwarfs have too, since their legs are very short compared to their upper bodies. I eat my meals in carefully measured portions, like people who have diabetes and other health problems. It's tough for me, because I like to pig out; but it's something I have to do.

One of my favorite activities at school is swimming, which is easy and a lot of fun—I just have to make sure to stay on my back so that I can breathe. Our pool is designed to have wheelchair access, and there are railings so we can get around more easily. I like track and field too, and I've participated in the Games for the Physically Challenged in swimming and track. In gym class at school they help us train for the games, and every June we all go to Nassau Community College to compete. I won three gold medals one year and four another year. I do the track events in my wheelchair, not on my legs.

Brooklyn is about an hour away from school. Every morning I get up at seven o'clock and wake up my father, who helps me dress and put on my legs. I have special stairs that I climb up to get into my wheelchair—the only thing I need is for someone to hold my hands

while I'm going up. If I'm in a big rush my father lifts me up and puts me in. And if we're running really late, I carry my legs to school with me on the bus and one of the therapists helps me get them on. When I get to school, I park my chair in the hallway and walk to my desk. It's a lot like my computer desk at home, except it's low, and has a lower chair so that I can sit down without too much help. They built me special stairs, like the ones I have at home, to help me get in and out of chairs more easily.

I have an assistant at school, but I try to do as much as I can on my own—it's better for me to be independent. In a couple of years, when I start high school, I'll be able to live at school part-time if I want to. They have housing there so that kids can get some practice doing more things by themselves.

One person I'm really close to is my pediatrician, Judy Wallin. She's a great person to be with. My mother's known her since she was pregnant with me, so I've known her my whole life. She was always there for my mother, and she's always there for me and my brother. When I need medicine, or when I just need someone to talk to, Judy is the one I go to first. She often comes to our house on Sunday, her day off, so she can visit with us.

I am really lucky because I have a wonderful family and friends. A lot of children with disabilities come from broken families, because one of the parents can't handle it and they say good-bye. I'm always around both my parents, so I'm very close to both of them. They help me out with things like getting dressed, washing my hair, and getting into my chair—it's part of everyday life for all of us. I think my mother is a little more patient about letting me try to do things myself, but basically they both treat me the same way they treat my little brother.

My brother Anthony is five years old, and he doesn't have a handicap. If he weren't around, I think my parents would probably pay too much attention to me and I would never learn to do anything for myself. He can be a real pain sometimes, but I remember that when I was an only kid, I felt very alone. One good thing about the way we get along is that we never get jealous of each other. I've never been envious of him for not having a disability, and he never gets upset that my parents pay lots of attention to me. In that way, we're lucky.

I'm also close to my cousins. When we go to visit them, my brother and I play catch with them and have a lot of fun. The only time things get a little weird is when my cousins have friends over who don't know me—not everyone in their neighborhood knows me and understands about my disability. I have a lot of friends there, but there are always some who just sit there and stare.

Sometimes when people meet people like me and my friends from school, they back away. I hate it when people feel afraid when they see me. It makes me sad when people meet me and they don't know what they're supposed to do. I think they should be just the way they are with anybody else—they should shake my hand and introduce themselves.

Joel Duggins

I'VE NEVER KNOWN WHAT it would be like to walk on my own two feet. I was born with no leg below the knee on my right side. I was only eight months old when I got my new leg—a prosthesis. I imagine it would be much harder to adjust to the situation if you were born with both legs and had to have one amputated later on.

I was also born with some birth defects in both my hands. My right hand was badly deformed and my left hand had a little webbing between the thumb and index finger. I had three or four operations to fix my fingers. Before that, I was using my hands like claws. I don't remember any of those surgeries because I was too young. My mom's told me the whole story though, and it's pretty interesting.

What happened, according to my mom, was that shortly after I was born the doctors told her it was too early to operate because my hands needed to grow. They said she should take me to a physical therapist twice a week, so that's what she did from the time I was two months old until I was one and a half. It cost a fortune because back then there weren't as many resources for the physically challenged. My parents couldn't get me into a program at the BHI, which is the Bureau for Handicapped Children, because my father was a fireman and made too much money for us to qualify for this kind of financial assistance. But firemen don't make all that much money, and my dad had to support a family of five. The private physical therapy sessions cost ninety dollars a pop, so we were spending a hundred and eighty dollars a week on them in addition to all the other money we had to pay every time we visited my doctor, an orthopedic surgeon named Dr. Leon Root.

When I was a year and a half old, Dr. Root suggested to my mom that we might save some money by going to the clinic at the Hospital for Special Surgery to see what could be done about my hand, so that's what we did. But the doctor there told her I would have a nonfunctional right hand. Mom simply refused to accept this prognosis and she marched up to another doctor she had heard a lot about because he's one of the top hand specialists in the country. His name is Dr. Richard McCormick and he said he could save at least three of my fingers. He ended up saving four. I originally had an index finger which was fused with my middle finger and it didn't work. Dr. McCormick unfused the two fingers and turned my index finger into a thumb. I also had one of the tendons taken out of my leg and grafted onto my new thumb.

Since Dr. McCormick was a private doctor, and the surgery wasn't part of the clinic program, my mother really had to struggle to make ends meet. She sold her jewelry and pawned a lot of her stuff so I could have the private care she wanted me to have. She says even if she has to work three jobs, she'll make sure I get proper medical care for as long as I need it. That's the kind of person she is. My birth defects have really been a financial burden on my family.

My leg's a different story. I've had three or four major operations on that, the most recent this past year. They are called stump revisions. My tibia bone was growing faster than the skin, and when that happens they have to shave down the bone. The surgeon who operates on my leg is Dr. Root and, like Dr. McCormick, he's with the Hospital for Special Surgery in New York City. I was in the hospital for three days, and then I had to miss school for over three months. I had a tutor at home and he came to see me two hours a day, five times a week. My teacher sent my homework home every day so I could keep up with my classmates.

I have two brothers, Tavey, who's twenty, and a twin brother, Jason, who was born totally normal. It may sound strange but I've never felt envious of Jason or given the matter much thought. I just figure

that God made me the way I am and that's how I am. I don't think of myself as being disabled because I can do anything that anyone else can do—play sports, run, jump, swim, ride a bike. I've never tried ice-skating but I have tried skiing with Paddy Rossbach's ASPIRE program and that was fun. I was rigged up on one ski which was attached to my normal leg and I took the prosthesis off my right leg. Then I used poles with little skis on the end of them which provide proper balance. They're called outriggers and it's like skiing on three skis. The first time I tried I won a gold medal in downhill racing. As a matter of fact, I've won lots of gold medals over the years in running, shotput, and javelin. I used to be very involved with Sports for the Physically Challenged, but I haven't been for the past two years because my schoolwork takes so much time.

I think that when you have a handicap, whatever it is, you should think of yourself as a real person. It's important that you don't try to live up to *other* people's standards. You should try not to join groups just because your friends want you to—or because they say, "You can't do it," and you join just to prove you can.

My mother says that when I was younger, I was a lot angrier. She remembers times when I got so mad I said stuff like "I wish I had never been born." It must have been when I came home after the last surgery. I may not remember getting mad, but I sure remember how much pain I felt. It lasted for about a week. It was so bad I cried, and I don't cry a lot.

My physical therapist is named Pat Marcus and she's been a big help teaching me how to walk with my prosthesis. No one, except my family and doctors, has seen my actual prosthesis. I'm very private about that. My two best friends, Dean and Craig, have seen me without my artificial leg attached—they came by to see me after my operation—but they haven't seen my prosthesis either. When I'm not wearing it I keep it in my mother's closet.

It's made out of plastic and metal and has a Flex-Foot so when I walk or run I look like anyone else. The Flex-Foot has made a big difference for me. It not only helps me walk with a better gait, but it's a lot quieter. And because I walk better and use my ankle more, my current prosthesis is more functional. Before I got my Flex-Foot, I wasn't as sure-footed as I am now. I remember one time when I was walking to get groceries from the car and my foot separated from the rest of my prosthesis. I took a bad tumble and luckily I wasn't hurt. But I was scared.

My prosthetist's name is John Cottrel. I go to see him about twice a year and he watches me walk up and down the hall to see if I need an adjustment. I oil the bolts on my artificial leg about three times a month to keep it from rusting. It's the same oil you use on doors to make sure they don't squeak or whatever.

The leg itself is kept in place with a thigh corset which is held together by using either Velcro or laces. I use laces because they provide extra therapy for my hands. There are foam and plastic suction cups inside the prosthesis which clamp on to the sides of my stump. It's crucial that I have a very secure fit because if I don't, the skin on the end of my stump, which is very thin and fragile, gets irritated and sore and this can turn into an infection. The reason the end of my stump is so thin-skinned is because the tibia bone inside my short leg has no idea that it's not growing inside a normal leg—so it just keeps on growing. And as long as my bones are growing I have to keep on having stump revisions so the bone won't penetrate my skin. Right now, we are hoping that my stump will hold out for two or three more years before I have to have another revision.

I go to see Dr. Root several times a year so he can check my stump and be sure I'm not abusing it. He's the person who decides if and when I need a revision. I like him because he understands my feelings and takes them into consideration. For example, after my last operation I couldn't wear my prosthesis for about three months. I either hopped or, once in a while, I used a wheelchair. Crutches aren't an option for me and it would be a waste of time for any doctor to prescribe them. Everyone who works with me finally realizes how I feel about this matter. Crutches make me feel more handicapped than I want to feel.

Fortunately, the question of crutches isn't usually an issue since I'm not having all that many operations. I wear my prosthesis most of the time and I just have to use common sense. One of the ways I avoid falling is by walking carefully and remembering to pick up my feet—not to be a lazy walker. And it's very important for me to do exercises so that both my legs are even. Right now, I'm quite lopsided because over the years I've hopped so much on my good leg that it's over-built-up, and my stump leg looks as if it's been in a sauna too long. I'm using leg weights on the stump side to build up those muscles. When my thigh fills out I'll look better, too, because even though I always wear pants, one leg's much skinnier than the other.

Being a guy has probably been an advantage for me with this particular disability for a number of reasons. One, I wear pants anyway, so lots of people don't even know I have a prosthesis. And secondly, guys my age aren't as concerned about their looks as girls are. I guess I should just talk for myself because when I think about it, some guys do care—like my brothers, who will spend hours in front of the mirror sheening their hair. But that's not my way.

As for my hands, they don't cause me much of a problem. Most people don't even notice I have only four fingers on my right hand. My left hand is less of a problem since there was only webbing between my thumb and index finger so that's fully functional now. Luckily I'm left-handed, for most things anyway. My mother says it's strange to watch me playing baseball because when I throw the

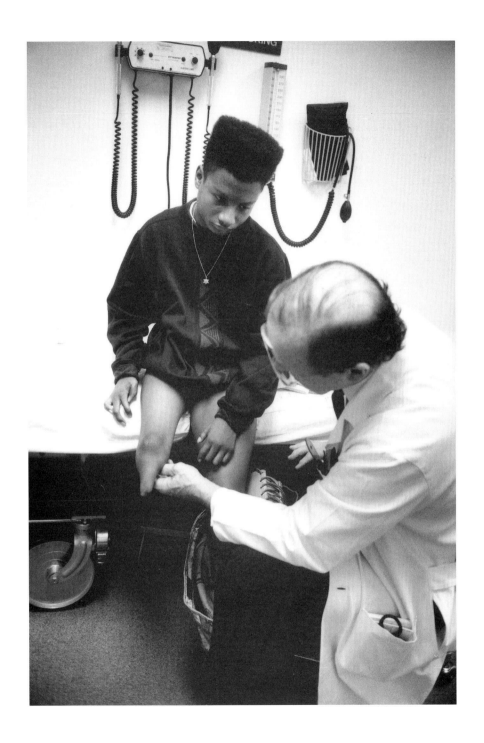

ball I'm left-handed, but when I bat I'm right-handed. Jason and I both play a lot of baseball and we both happen to play the same position—left field. He's in the Little League but I'm not. It's not because I couldn't be if I wanted to; it's just not my preference. I'm very sports-oriented and my hands have never caused me a problem, even when the sport involves catching a ball. The only time I feel self-conscious or embarrassed is when I meet new people or go to church, because then I have to shake hands and I know they're noticing. But I try not to care.

Even though I live a normal life, I often dream that I'm playing baseball or walking somewhere and my leg has fallen off. Whenever I have this dream, I wake up right away because it scares me. But as long as I'm awake, I don't think about it a whole lot. Lots of people don't even know I wear a prosthesis because I never wear shorts. If they don't ask me, I don't tell them. When I was younger, I used to tell people that I was just wearing a brace and they believed me. I did this because I was young and having a prosthesis embarrassed me. It still embarrasses me a little—but not as much as it used to. If my friends ask me now what's the matter, I tell them the truth, even though it's none of their business. I certainly don't go around telling people I have an artificial leg. For me, it's a personal matter.

I'm getting somewhat more open about my leg, but I still remember the first time I went swimming. After I had changed into my swimsuit and removed my prosthesis, I was so self-conscious and in such a hurry to get into the pool that I completely forgot one very important matter. I didn't know how to swim and I sank like a rock! Our group leader had to dive in and fish me out. I learned how to swim very quickly after that!

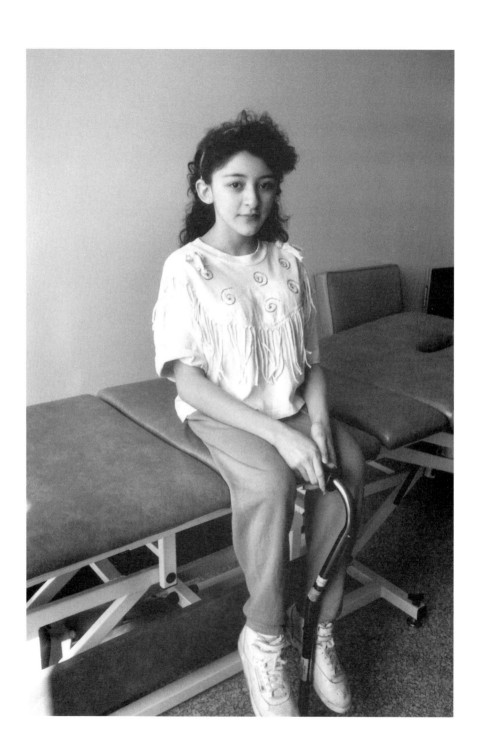

Melissa Medrano

AGE THIRTEEN

I WAS BORN WITH both of my legs broken. When my parents took me home from the hospital, they noticed that I always kept my legs bunched up. In the beginning they didn't realize anything was wrong, but when I started screaming with pain every time they changed my diaper, they got worried. They took me to the doctor right away.

At first, the doctors thought my parents were abusing me, but then they did some tests and found out that I had a rare bone disease called osteogenesis imperfecta. It's a genetic disease, and it means that my bones don't use calcium the way other people's bones do. This makes them very brittle and soft, so they break easily.

After I was diagnosed, I spent about two months in the hospital with my legs in plaster of paris casts. When I came home, my parents were extremely careful when they handled me, and they made sure

I didn't bump myself on anything. The hardest time was when I was learning to walk. If my mother didn't watch me constantly, I would try to stand up on my own and I'd usually fall down and break something. I broke about twenty bones before I was seven years old. One time, my leg broke just because I was sitting down the wrong way.

Breaking a bone is awful. It feels like a whole bunch of knives going into you. The funny thing is, at first you don't really feel the pain because you're in shock—you feel like you're flying through the air. But after you get hit with the pain, you start having spasms. Then you have to be rushed to the hospital. Once, a bone came right through my skin after it broke! The doctors put some medicine on my leg to numb it. Then they put the bone back where it belonged and casted up my leg. It was very scary.

I had my first operation when I was seven. My left femur, the big bone that goes from my hip to my knee, had broken in several places, so they took it out and put a metal rod inside it. I've had nine surgeries since, all to put rods in my legs. The rods act as braces—they help me stand up and they prevent my bones from breaking so easily. The weird thing about having the rods in my bones is that on rainy or cloudy days my legs start aching like crazy, and I can't go to school because it hurts so much.

When I had my first surgery, I was in the hospital for two weeks. Then I had to stay in bed with a cast on my leg for about six weeks afterwards. Because of the surgery, my right leg is shorter than my left, so they had to build up the bottom of my sneaker to make up the difference. Nowadays, I'm used to the operations and to the hospital—they've pretty much become a part of my life.

I can't wait until I stop growing, because then I won't need so many operations to replace the rods. Whenever one of my legs outgrows a rod, the doctors have to make an incision in my leg and put in a longer rod. It's easy to tell when I need a new rod because it begins to press against the nerves in my bone, which hurts like crazy. I'll need to be operated on at least two or three more times before I stop growing.

Not only do I have to spend a week or two in the hospital every time I get a new rod, but sometimes I have to stay in for rehabilitation. The last rehab took three months. It's not easy to be away from home for so long, especially because I don't get to see my family much. My parents both take a lot of interest in me, but they both work very hard at their jobs and my mother is at school studying to be a nurse. Unless I've just had an operation, I usually only get to see my mom and dad when they take me home on weekends. Luckily, the therapists at the hospital are really caring. They help whenever someone has a problem, and if I'm alone they keep me company.

On an average day of rehab, I get up around seven, eat, and head for the swimming pool. I have about four sessions of physical therapy, two sessions of occupational therapy, and maybe two hours of school every day. They keep us pretty busy!

A lot of my physical therapy takes place in the walking tank. This is a big whirlpool full of warm water. I get in there and they give me a set of exercises to do. Usually it's a little too hot, but after I've done my exercises they let me do whatever I want, like playing volleyball in the water, or just swimming.

Swimming is the best exercise for me because even if I fall, I can't really hurt myself. It also helps me to build strength. In the summer, when I'm more active, I notice that I'm a lot stronger. My doctor tells me that the more exercise I get, the less trouble my bones will have absorbing calcium.

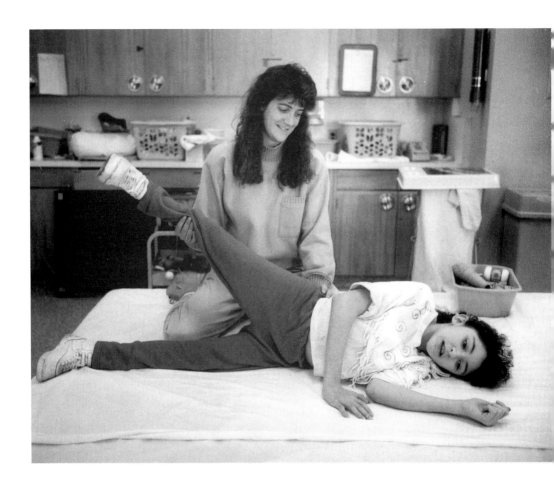

In occupational therapy I work with my hands and arms. I don't really need to do "OT"; it mainly keeps me busy. But other kids need it to get strong. I learn a lot from the other kids on my floor, like what different kinds of diseases can do to you. Sometimes when I find out how badly off the other kids are, I feel relatively lucky.

My physical therapist's name is Cheryl Paulson. I work with her two or three times a day and we do exercises like side leg lifts, sit-ups, and riding an exercise bike. She is really cool and fun to be with, and if I ever have a problem I know I can go and talk to her about it. She is one of the people who make staying at rehab a little easier.

Between the broken bones, the surgeries and the rehabs, I've been in the hospital around forty times since I was a baby. When I go in, I have a lot of people to say hello to. I'm pretty close to some of the nurses, since they're around a lot more than the doctors. Being around there so much has made me want to be a pediatrician when I grow up. I'd like to work with children, and I think it would be very rewarding to be a surgeon or to work in a clinic.

The bad thing about spending all this time in the hospital is that I miss a ton of school. This makes keeping up with my friends and my homework difficult. I work hard on schoolwork when I'm in the hospital. They have a classroom and a very nice teacher, and the teachers at my school are very understanding. They get my assignments together for me and then my mother picks them up and brings them over to me. Ever since I was eight, I've been in the class for gifted students. The good thing about having to stay off my feet all the time is that I have plenty of time to study.

Besides missing school, one of the worst things about being in the hospital all the time is having no privacy. Dr. Bernstein, who has been taking care of me since I was a baby and who performs all my operations, listens to me and I know he cares about all his patients. But some doctors are just rude. Sometimes, they walk into my room without knocking when I'm dressing. I tell them nicely to get out, and they usually get embarrassed and apologize. One time, my doctor brought a whole group of residents into my room without any warning. I talked to him about it, and now he gives me lots of notice if he's bringing people to see me.

The other time when I don't get along with the residents that well is when I'm in pain. For example, when something hurts I usually try not to show it. I like to be out with my friends and doing stuff, not lying in bed, so I always make an effort to keep my mind off the pain. The problem is, when I do say I feel pain and I need medication, some of the residents think I'm kidding. They're not like Dr. Bernstein and the nurses, who know me and can tell when I'm having a problem. The residents expect me to be lying down and crying when it hurts, and I don't like anyone to see me that way.

I don't spend all my time in the hospital. When I'm not at home, I love to stay active and hang out with my family and friends. I like to cheer on my friends when they do sports at school, even though I'm a little envious that I can't play too. Instead, I exercise with my Richard Simmons tape and take evening walks. Also, we have a really nice neighbor, who lets me swim in her pool when I want to.

For the past two summers my sister and I have gone to a camp for children with disablities. There are lots of activities there—horseback riding, swimming, nature hikes, and art. At nighttime, we go to coed dances or see movies. It's fun. Best of all, they have sponsors like the *Los Angeles Times* newspaper, which donates a lot of money so my parents don't have to spend a fortune to send us there.

That's lucky because between me and my sister, my parents have a lot of medical expenses. Christina is ten years old and she has osteogenesis imperfecta, too. After my parents had me, they knew that if they had another child it would have a fifty-fifty chance of having the same disease. They decided to have Christina anyway, because they didn't want me to be an only child. I'm glad they did it, because now I have a very nice and caring sister.

When my parents go out, they have to train our baby-sitters first, since Christina or I could have a problem at any time. They always let us know where they're going to be, and for how long. So far, we've never had an emergency when my parents were out. In fact, I've never had to go to the hospital in an ambulance. One of my parents has always been around to drive me there.

Christina doesn't have the disease as badly as I do, but I think she has a harder time dealing with it. Sometimes when she breaks a leg, she says she wishes she weren't alive. I tell her she'll get over it, that she won't always feel that way. I think that getting through all my operations has given me a lot of courage, and I'm trying to pass it along to her.

I think the other thing that gives me strength is being a Christian. I try to go to church every Sunday, and it does make me feel stronger. When I'm in church, I pray for God to give me the courage to stand the operations and everything that's ahead of me, and I pray that I won't break any more bones.

Recently, Dr. Bernstein told me I'll need to walk with a cane for the next year and a half or so. Since I haven't broken a bone in two years, he wants to make sure I don't lose my balance and break a leg. Even though my disease is getting better with time, I'm not very independent. My knees and waist are weak, so I need to use a long pole with a clamper attached to the end to pick things up from the floor. We call it my picker-upper. Also, when I take a shower, I need help getting in and out. The hospital is ordering me a special bath chair to make things easier, since now I usually sit on the shower floor.

The disease has also affected my hearing, since the ear is made up of tiny bones. The bones in my ear are much softer and weaker than other people's and they break a lot more easily. The doctors have told me that by the time I'm thirty there's a chance I'll be half deaf. I'm a little worried about it, but I don't always believe everything the doctors tell me.

I'd like to get married someday, and once I asked my doctor about having a baby. He said there would be a fifty-fifty chance of my child having osteogenesis imperfecta. I don't think I'd want to take that chance, so I'd rather adopt when the time comes.

In the fall, I'm starting high school. I'm excited, because I feel like it will be the beginning of a whole new life. It makes me feel good to know that I've come as far as I have with my disease, and that things can only get better for me in the years ahead.

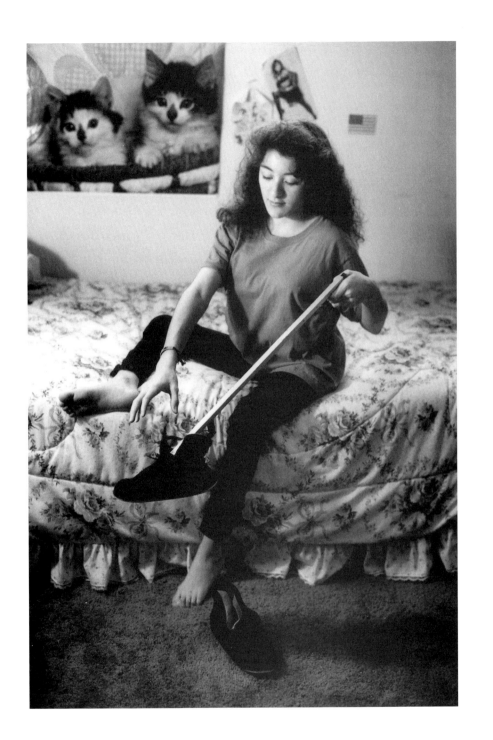

Recently I developed and was diagnosed with lordosis, which means the lower part of my back has started to curve inward. Now I have to wear a back brace to keep my back as straight as possible—so it won't curve in any more than it does right now. I don't like wearing the brace but it stops my back pain and keeps me comfortable. I asked my doctor what he can do to straighten my back and he said the only thing he could do is to take me back to surgery and do a spinal fusion. A spinal fusion is an operation in which my doctor opens my back and inserts a metal rod along my spine to keep my back straight. The metal rods are like the rods my doctor puts in my legs. I'm scared to death to go through this surgery because I don't know what to expect after I come back from the operating room. I'm afraid that some of my nerves will get damaged and then I'll become paralyzed. But then I tell myself that I have an excellent and skilled doctor and he wouldn't let that happen to me. I guess I'm mostly afraid of what the pain will feel like after the surgery and what my physical limits will be, since I have never experienced this kind of surgery before. I realize that in order to get this challenge over with I should just be positive and pray for courage and for the Lord to be by my side the whole time.

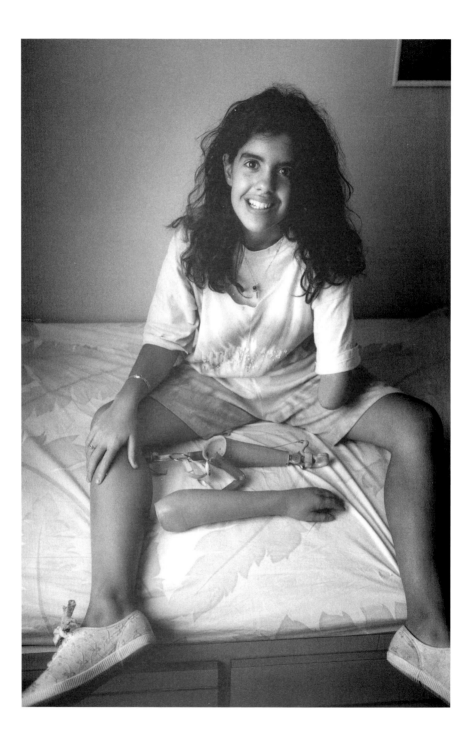

Michelle Fernandez

AGE FIFTEEN

ALL MY LIFE I have been different from everyone else. The reason is that I'm missing my left hand. Living life without a hand is just a little inconvenient. Instead of doing things with two hands, I do them with one.

For as long as I can remember, my parents, my sister Cary, and all my cousins, aunts, uncles, grandparents, and friends have given me lots of love and support. When I was younger, my parents treated me like a normal kid. Except they didn't want me to look different— not because they didn't accept me the way I was, but because they didn't want others to make fun of me. They wanted me to wear a prosthesis—a fake hand, which caused a lot of conflict between us because I never liked to wear one. It just isn't me. It took a while but my parents finally agreed that if I didn't want to wear a prosthesis I didn't have to. Now that they've gotten used to the idea, they prefer to see me without a fake hand. They feel I can do things better without one. My mom says that when I wear my prosthesis, I look

as though my entire left side is paralyzed because I move in a different way. In my family, we call my left arm *brazito,* which is Spanish for "short arm." We're Cuban.

When I was smaller, I wasn't concerned about my hand. But now that I'm older, I think more about it. Sometimes I wonder if I will ever get married. I wonder if I will ever find a man who will love me and not care about my arm. I definitely want to have children, and so I wonder if I will be a good mother. I guess the answers to all those thoughts will be found out in the future. For now, I try to concentrate on my daily life.

I try to live my life one day at a time. As a normal human being, I have good days and bad days. There are even days when I get home from school and I cry. Crying makes me feel better. I have never had a problem in letting my emotions show. When I feel sad, I cry and try to get happy again. My parents have always taught me that it's good to express your feelings. They support me by giving me love. My mother is always there for me when I need her. My father always gives me advice about life and lends me a helping hand.

My sister Cary is great. She's always pushing me to do things I thought I could never do because I was missing a hand. One day she and her boyfriend Steve were going to go waterskiing, and they invited me to come with them. I told them I would try it and my sister said, "Of course you will!" For my first time, I did very well. Cary is a wonderful sister. She tells her friends that the only real difference between us is I have five nails to paint instead of ten and one wrist to put bracelets on instead of two.

My friends make a big difference in how I feel about myself. Jessica says that most of the time she forgets I have a missing hand. I've known Suzy for over nine years and she's one of my closest friends who is always there for me. She says it's hard to believe that I only have five fingers, because I can do everything she can do and do it just as well. Another friend, Tatiana, has taught me that even if you are physically whole, you're still not perfect.

I don't really have any close guy friends, except for José Fernandez. Even though we have the same last name, we're not related in any way. I met him last summer and found him to be someone I could talk to. When I first met him, I wasn't sure if he had noticed my missing hand. Usually when I first meet people, I can notice right away when they realize I have only one hand. With José it was different. He only seemed aware of my *feelings*.

I think the hardest part of living life without a hand is when it comes to meeting new people. It isn't that I'm afraid of meeting new people, but I always wonder what they think of me when they first see me. Twice in my life I've been introduced to someone who didn't even notice that I was different—that I was missing a hand. One time, the person thought I was hiding my lower arm inside my shirtsleeve. Another time, when I was about eight years old, we went to an Eckerd drugstore on Halloween to buy some orange spray paint to put on my hair. When we went to pay for it, the cashier said, "Oh, my God, what a great outfit! How did you do it?" I was dressed like a punk rocker. I thought he was talking about my costume, but he was looking at my *brazito* and he thought it was a trick—like I was *very* punk. He kept asking me how I did it and I kept saying, "Did what?" Then we realized he was talking about my arm and my dad explained I was born that way. The guy was so embarrassed his face turned bright red!

What bothers me the most—and it hurts me a lot—is when people feel pity for me. I consider myself a normal person who is physically independent. I get annoyed and angry when people offer to do things for me that I can do by myself. I force myself to do things to prove that I can do them even though I'm missing a hand.

When I was younger, my dad went to the library to see if he could find any books for children with handicaps. The only one he came up with was called *The One-Hander's Book* by Veronica Washam. It was mostly for grown-ups and had hints about how to light a match or how to pay tolls when you're driving. My favorite page was in the beginning where there was a definition from *Webster's Dictionary* of a handicap. It said:

> "Handicap—a race or contest . . . in which in order
> to equalize chances of winning an artificial disadvan-
> tage is imposed on a supposedly superior contestant."

Of course, it's probably a lot easier for me to live in today's world with all its electronic pencil sharpeners, computers, push-button car windows, and remote controls. But it's still important that I learn

how to do things so I'm dependent on myself and not on technology. I'm luckier than most one-handed people because my left arm extends to just below the elbow and it's still very functional. And my right arm, since it's always performed double duty, is very strong. Sometimes in school when we have to do pull-ups in gym, I'm able to keep up with my classmates by using one arm. My phys-ed teachers have often tried to discourage me from even trying, and this frustrates me. I feel I should do whatever I feel I'm up to. I'm sure there are lots of times I try to do things that are a little too hard just to prove them wrong. And then I end up surprising myself because I can do everything I set my mind to doing. Sometimes it's been helpful when people have said I couldn't do something, because it forced me to try.

I learned to tie my shoelaces when I was six and a half and how to

ride a two-wheeler bike when I was seven. There are really only two things I can think of that I can't do. One is to put on earrings for pierced ears. Those little backings are just too tiny to deal with, and I don't like clip-ons because they hurt my ears—so my mom or my sister help me with those. I can wear the hoops for pierced ears— the kind that are all one piece without the separate backings—but there's no need to limit my choices as long as I'm living with other people. I have trouble with bracelets and necklaces too, but I just keep them on when I sleep or take a shower or swim. It's easier.

The other thing that's really hard for me is cutting meat, especially steak, but that's not a big deal. If I'm with my family or close friends, I don't have a problem asking them to help me. As for getting dressed, I do my bra or the top of my bathing suit by fastening it first and putting it over my head. I take it off the same way. Shirts with a lot of buttons in the back could be a problem but I button them first, except for the top three buttons, and then put my head through the top. I can't shuffle cards but if we're playing a game I let the other player do the shuffling, so it's no big deal.

I can always sense that people are staring at me, but it doesn't bother me anymore because I'm used to it. It doesn't mean I like it—only that I'm used to it. I know they have fancy prosthetics now, and I saw a program on "Donahue" about electric ones, but I doubt I'll ever be interested. I'm used to being the way I am.

My advice to people who meet someone like me is to treat them like a normal human being. Always remember that no human being in this world is perfect. A person might physically look different, but we are all equal inside.

I asked my mother, my father, and my sister to write down their feelings about me, and this is what they said.

JORGE, FATHER:

Michelle's birth without her left hand was an awakening for me. My first reaction was of deep pain, because I perceived it as a very negative condition. She would suffer greatly throughout life having a disadvantage. It was a pain that was not really very clear, because she was healthy in every other way. But I guess because she was physically imperfect, it was not acceptable to me. I am convinced now that Michelle has provided an awareness and acceptance to all kinds of human varieties that has enhanced my sensitivity as a human being.

My wife Silvia and my daughters Cary and Michelle have contributed greatly to my personal growth. My feelings toward Michelle's condition have always been of acceptance. I haven't been totally thrilled with it, but comfortable with the new awareness that it has brought into my life. Michelle has provided the opportunity for me to get in touch with my real feelings. For example, now I am able to cry and laugh more spontaneously and be more honest with myself. The experience of having to deal with her condition has made me more understanding of the process of living and the ongoing lessons of life.

SILVIA, MOTHER:

The day of Michelle's birth was the hardest day of my life, because I had a lot of different feelings about it. I felt mad, sad, hopeless—all the prenatal care that I had and now I couldn't do anything—and worried about her growing up without a hand.

But I made a decision a few days later. I will raise her the same way that I was raising her sister Cary, who was six years old at the time; and we did. She learned how to swim when she was three and a half, to tie her shoes when she was six and a half, to ride a bike without training wheels when she was seven, and now at fifteen she is getting her restricted driver's license to learn how to drive.

I am very proud of Michelle. She is like the sunshine of our house. She is always talking—she is very communicative—and laughing. She loves to go shopping with me on Saturdays. I think we have a very good mother-daughter relationship.

Sometimes, I worry about her meeting a man who will accept her. But at the same time, I am sure that she will. He will see the whole human being that she is—responsible, loving, caring, honest—and will love her as much as we do.

My advice to any expecting parents is that if they should find out before birth that their baby is missing a limb, please have it and give her or him a lot of love and support, and I am sure that they will never regret it.

CARY, SISTER:

I never really think of my sister as different because she has one hand rather than two. In fact, there have been times when I have been out with her and I notice that people are watching us and I think to myself, "What are they looking at?" Then later, I remember Michelle's arm and realize that is what they are interested in. It doesn't really bother me that people are curious, as long as they don't go overboard in staring.

As we both have grown up, I feel that I have become closer to Michelle. Our age difference—I am six years older than her—doesn't seem as large now as it once was, and we have more in common than ever. As we have become older, I have also come to admire Michelle more and more. This year she started high school, which is an exciting yet somewhat intimidating experience for everyone. But as she always does, Michelle handled the transition well and by the end of the year had made many new friends and, judging from the number of phone calls she gets every day, has become quite popular.

Michelle is very friendly and outgoing, and she never lets the fact that she is missing a hand stop her from trying anything. Perhaps because she is so daring and friendly it is so easy to forget about her hand. She really leads a normal life and manages to do everything, from tying her shoes to typing her reports, with one hand. If there is anything that upsets me about having a sister who is missing a hand, it is not anything directly related to her but rather the way others sometimes treat her. I hate it when well-meaning people assume she can't do things for herself and lower their demands for her or force their help on her when she doesn't need it. My advice to people who encounter someone like Michelle is to treat her as they would treat anyone, because she is as normal as you or me.

Francis Smith

AGE SIXTEEN

IF PEOPLE EVER ASK me what's wrong with me, I simply tell them that I was born with a genetic disorder. The technical name for what I have is Treacher Collins. Some people call it missing bones.

I was born without a chin, and since I had no chin there was no place for my tongue—that just hung out of my mouth—so I had to have a tracheotomy in order to breathe. I had no palate—that means the roof of my mouth was missing, and that had to be repaired surgically when I was about six.

I had no cheekbones, so my eyes were drooping because there was nothing to hold them in place. I had an operation to build them when I was about eight. For this procedure, they used bones from my ribs, because that's the one part of your body that will grow back again.

I was also born without outer ears. Instead, I had what looked like two tiny knobs on either side of my head. To correct this problem, I had five operations in which the plastic surgeon was able to make me a pair by using some of my cartilage from other parts of my body. The only problem is that there is nothing but solid bone connecting my outer ears to the inner nerves which make it possible for a person to hear, so I have to use a bone-conduction hearing aid.

Four years ago, they made a hole in the left side of my head and implanted what looks like a magnet so that I can attach a hearing aid onto the tiny disk which is implanted just above my left ear. I was the first child in the Midwest who tried this medical invention. Before they gave me the implant, I used to have to wear the hearing aid on a headband and everyone thought I was a little girl.

Even though I can hear well enough to carry on a conversation, the trouble is that sometimes I hear more than I want to. The small transmitter box which I wear and which magnifies sounds and sends them into my earpiece also picks up a lot of background noise too. As a consequence, I'm very uncomfortable in a crowded room with lots of people talking in the background. And it will make driving a car difficult for me because I'll have a hard time differentiating between the person who's directly behind me honking the horn and all the other street noises from farther away.

I'm ninety percent blind in my right eye and I can't read with that eye at all. I tried wearing glasses but they didn't help much. Sometimes I wear them when I do sports, but that's only to protect my good eye.

Even though they repaired my cleft palate, I still have a serious speech impairment, as well as an eating impairment. I have trouble chewing because only two teeth on each side of my mouth—one top and one bottom on each side, the ones in the very back of my mouth—come together when I bite. I can't eat apples, candy, meat, or most vegetables. As a result, I'm much thinner than I should be and have a hard time maintaining my weight. Solid foods present a real problem for me. One time I ended up in the emergency room at the hospital because I choked on a piece of sausage. It was on Mother's Day. My orthodontist and my craniofacial doctor are working together as a team to try to align my teeth and, in the process, extend my chin. I've been wearing braces on my teeth for a year and a half and have surgery planned in the fall so I'll have an easier time eating. So far I have had at least twenty-five operations, but to tell you the truth, I've lost count and so have my parents.

My parents are wonderful. I started living with them when I was two and a half years old. My birth parents were both teachers from Ireland who were traveling in the United States when I was born. They felt they couldn't cope with my severe medical problems and transferred me right from the hospital to a foster home when I was only a few days old. I was taken care of by an elderly black woman until the Smiths heard about me. What happened is that Betty and Bob, who are now my parents, went to a seminar that was being held for caseworkers who specialized in placing children. Because Betty and Bob had already adopted several children with special needs, they were asked to speak about their experiences. After the seminar was over, the director went up to Betty and said, "I've already found a home for one of our children." Betty said, "That's wonderful, but how could you have done it so fast?" The director said, "It's you!" And that's when the director told them all about me and why she thought I would fit right into their family.

Betty and Bob agreed, and I've been with them ever since. They legally adopted me about two years ago. They're the most incredible people you can imagine. They have adopted a total of ten children with special needs. They had one biological child, Andy, who is in his forties, but we don't know where he is. He fought in the Vietnam

157

War and he's been missing in action since that time. We know he's alive but that's the only information we have. My dad, who is sixty-six, is retired now—he used to be a mechanical engineer for Magnavox—and my mom just celebrated her sixty-first birthday. They still have twice as much energy as people half their age.

Most of my brothers and sisters are quite a lot older than I am, and a lot of them are grown up, married, and living on their own. There are only five of us living at home. Besides me, there are Robert and Raymond, who are twenty-five-year-old twins, who were both born with serious facial deformities as well as with learning disabilities. They look fine now as a result of multiple operations and they both have jobs. Raymond works at a learning center as a patient trainee, and Robert is a manager of a group home for people with emotional and learning disabilities. Megan, who is twenty-one, is learning dis-

abled and she does assembly work. The youngest member of our family is Ruth. She's eleven. As a result of severe meningitis when she was a baby, she lost her legs above the knee, a finger on her right hand, and much of her nose. She also suffered severe skin disfigurement. She had such a high fever that it burned away a lot of her skin tissue. She uses artificial legs, and sometimes a wheelchair, to get around.

Four members of our family are living on their own. My brother Thaddeus, who is twenty-seven, was born with a severe case of cerebral palsy and uses crutches to get around. Thad has a degree is psychology and now works as the director for volunteers of Hospice in Fort Wayne, Indiana. Mary is thirty-five and she has epilepsy. She's married and living with her husband and their three children. Joselynn is also married and has three children. She has asthma. In 1982, my brother Peter, the son of migrant workers, who was born with rickets, died in an automobile accident when he was twenty. And my brother Jamie, the son of a heroin-addicted mother, is now serving time in prison because of the resulting behavioral problems. But through it all, the good times and the bad, my family has been a close-knit, supportive unit.

My parents have fought battles for medical care, decent education, and social acceptance for all of us. There never seems to be a problem which they can't face with strength and a sense of humor. For example, just finding a house big enough for all of us was a real challenge. Here's what happened: We live in a small town in Garrett, Indiana, and there used to be two funeral homes. The funeral directors were always competing against one another and there wasn't all that much business. So one of them bought the other one out. The funeral director who got bought out needed to sell his funeral parlor, but he couldn't find anyone who needed a house with fourteen rooms and, on top of that, no one wanted to buy a house that had been a funeral home. They thought it was too creepy.

After the place had been on the market for a while, the funeral director, who had heard about my family, talked to my parents and said, "Why don't you make an offer of what you can afford to pay?" Even though my parents' bid was ridiculously low, he accepted it because he wanted us to have the house and put it to good use. As it turned out, besides having fourteen rooms, there are lots of elevators in the back of the house which used to be for bringing the caskets in and out, so it's totally accessible for anyone on crutches or in a wheelchair. My mother's favorite line is that "it took a family like ours to bring life into the old funeral parlor!"

Besides the loving, tender care of my parents and my brothers and sisters, my church has been an important factor in my life. I now belong to Bible Baptist Church in Auburn, Indiana. The pastor, my Sunday school teachers, and my fellow church members have been a real blessing, especially their prayer support around the times of my frequent surgeries.

My school has also made me happy inside, but it wasn't always that way. Today, I attend Canterbury School in Fort Wayne, Indiana, and its academic program is very rigorous and challenging. They have a generous financial aid program and I got in on a full scholarship. My classmates are cheerful, loving, and caring kids. They encourage me and help me with my homework in math and science-related things. Last year, I was the manager of my basketball team, and this year I'm going to be doing a lot of camera work for the team, videotaping the players so they can see themselves play and improve their strategy. I feel that my classmates accept me for who I am and that I'm in an environment where my intelligence is respected. But as I said, it hasn't always been that way for me.

Before I switched over to Canterbury, my life at school was a living hell. Mostly I went to public schools. The kids were heavily into Satanic worship, rock music, and word-search games. I wasn't, and as a result I didn't fit in anywhere. At first, my peers just picked on me, chipping away at my self-esteem with verbal harassing. I felt deeply hurt inside and tried to find an inner strength to get me through the days.

But then life got a lot worse. Spit wads, peashooters, and other makeshift weapons became the rage, the ultimate tools of harassment. Verbal abuse still accompanied the physical abuse. The kids would sneak up on me and launch a spit wad, taking pleasure at my reactions. They called me names. They would snap me on the shoulder with their fingers. My locker was often raided and things were taken from it. Or it was filled with shaving cream.

I felt fear every time I walked into a classroom, the school library, the band room, the cafeteria, and through the corridors. In the band room, they would corner me or lock me in one of the smaller rooms. One day, in junior high, a bunch of students cornered me and began hitting my head against the lockers. Most of the time I felt like a walking dead person. Sometimes I cried. I couldn't bear to tell my parents, because they would worry about me and I felt I could handle it myself.

Even though I was hurt and scared inside, there wasn't anything they could do to ruin my schoolwork. When I was sitting in the classroom, I still managed to pay attention and participate and I did my best in the school band because I love music. I made straight As in every class and made the honor roll every year. No matter how mean and violent the kids were to me, God kept me sane. But now that I'm away from what was a living hell, I realize, looking back, that what happened to me is that I was hurt so much that I buried most of my feelings. I have learned to be more outgoing and to come out of my shell. My acceptance at Canterbury has helped my feelings about myself.

I also feel better when I'm out in public—grocery shopping, traveling, stuff like that. I do not mind being stared at by anyone. I just ignore it and go about my business because now that I have so many friends, my self-esteem is like an invisible shield encompassing my entire being.

There has been one other important contributing factor to my well-being—in addition to all the help I've received from my family, my church, my new school friends, and my doctors. For the past two summers, I've been lucky enough to go to Camp About Face, which was organized by Riley Children's Hospital. All the children who go there have craniofacial defects. Some have a cleft lip and palate, which is the most common facial defect. Some of the campers have more severe problems such as Crouzon's syndrome and Apert's syn-

drome, which are birth anomalies that affect the whole face as well as the shape of the head. It's the one time of the year when I get to be with kids who have all experienced what I have—the surgeries, the speech difficulties, and the stigma of looking different. This past summer there were twenty-two of us, including my sister Ruth.

The camp is located in southern Indiana, in Bradford Woods, on a big lake. We all stay in cabins and the counselors are really nice. Most of them are college students who are majoring in recreation or child development. Besides playing games and doing the usual camp activities like hiking, swimming, and canoeing, we spend part of each day with various members of the staff from Riley. The speech pathologists work with us to improve our speech, the dentists talk to us about taking care of our teeth, and the plastic surgeons examine us and then tell us how we can further improve our appearance through plastic surgery. Mainly, they ask us if there's anything that bothers us about our appearance, and if there is, they tell us what can be done to improve it.

There's a child psychiatrist who talks with us about our expectations and helps us differentiate between those that are realistic and those that aren't. She also gives us tips on how to handle teasing and build our self-esteem. There are hairstyling and makeup lessons. I didn't bother with those lessons, because I think people in our society pay too much attention to the Hollywood look. What's important is what's inside your heart.

But I did work very hard in the session devoted to ways we could improve our speech. Some things I already knew, like speaking slower so people can understand me better. Trish Severns, the craniofacial coordinator of the camp, who is also a speech pathologist, worked with me quite a bit. She checked out the configuration of my oral structures and the impact they have on my speech. She listened to my articulation and tested me in various ways, like pinching my nostrils while I talked to see if there was air coming out of my nose while I spoke. She talked to me about the speech therapy I had at school and about things the craniofacial team doctors and speech therapists can do to better understand my speech problems, or the nature of my speech, or my speech status. She arranged for me to come into the hospital after camp to have a special speech X ray called a videofluoroscopy where the doctors can actually see my palate, or oral structures, moving on a TV screen while I'm talking. This way, they can determine if further surgery will improve my voice.

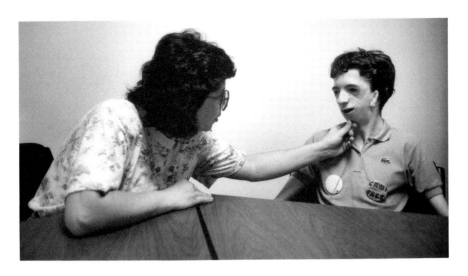

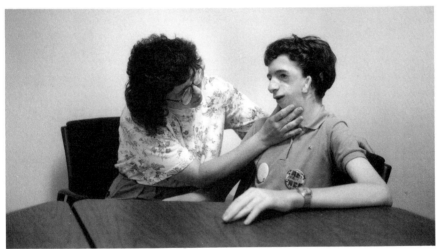

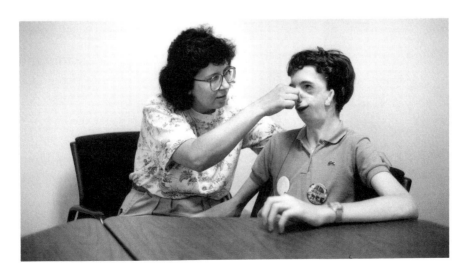

One of the programs that I particularly enjoyed at camp was Partners Night. There's a beach party on the lake and some adults with facial defects who have been through what we're going through now were invited to visit camp and talk with us. I spent the whole evening talking with a guy named John Smyser who, like me, was born with

Treacher Collins syndrome. He's thirty-five, and he told me that when he was born they didn't even have a name for the disease. They figured he was a mess and retarded too, and the doctors wanted to institutionalize him. But his parents kept him and did a great job raising him. First, he went to a deaf-oral school but then he was mainstreamed. By the time he was sixteen he had gone through twenty-six operations and then he said, "Enough!" because by then he had other priorities like debating and track.

John told me all about his job with Pitney Bowes. He's a specialist in the service department and has sixteen people working under him. He's been with the company for eleven years. He showed me pictures of his wife and two children and it was obvious that he's got a great life for himself. His kids don't even notice that he's different—they don't give it a second thought. He said there was no reason why I couldn't have a wonderful future. What he told me was, "You just have to go through life saying, 'Hi, I'm me, and this is the way I am, and once people get to know you they'll say, 'No big deal!' "

I hope I can return to camp next summer. And I hope Ruthie will return, too. We had a wonderful time. I made a lot of new friends. It may be called Camp About Face, but what I really experienced was the inner me.

I FIRST MET PADDY ROSSBACH through Elizabeth Bonwich, one of the subjects of my previous book, *How It Feels to Fight for Your Life*. Paddy was running a program called ASPIRE at the Hospital for Special Surgery in New York City, and also working with patients at the Memorial Sloan-Kettering Cancer Center on a consultant basis. The ASPIRE program combines psychosocial support and aggressive rehabilitation for amputees of all ages, but Paddy is also involved with many individuals who have not had an amputation but who do have a limb deficiency.

One of the reasons that Paddy has such a good rapport with her patients is because she is an amputee herself. She has never allowed it to stop her from doing everything she wants to do. She trained as a nurse in her native England, met her husband scuba-diving, she skis, competes with the able-bodied on her horse in dressage, and holds the women's amputee record for both the New York City and London marathons. While still associated with both the above hospitals, she is presently pursuing an independent career within the same field.

I asked Paddy about the importance of sports for children with disabilities and the organizations that support them. This is her reply.

J. K.

A Letter
from Paddy Rossbach

Most people assume that sports are not for children with disabilities, and yet participation in, and excelling at, a sport is one of the best ways of building self-confidence and self-esteem, and the training not only improves performance, but improves balance, coordination, concentration, circulation, muscle strength, and, of course, the way one's body looks.

Today there are international, national, and local athletic organizations for each disability. All of them have junior divisions and are working hard to put on teaching clinics, as well as competitive events in a large variety of sports. The national organizations are divided into the following groups, for individuals

- who have amputations
- who are blind
- who have cerebral palsy
- who are hearing impaired

- who have spinal-cord injuries
- who have dwarfism
- who do not fit into any of the above categories, such as multiple sclerosis, muscular dystrophy, and others.

These are exciting times. We are starting to focus on our abilities rather than our disabilities. Both junior and senior athletes who excel earn the right to represent their country in international events, competing on an equal level with athletes from other countries. In addition, many athletes are competing in able-bodied events.

The following is a list of the national disabled sports organizations. I urge everyone to become a member of the appropriate group:

National Handicapped Sports (NHS) (for amputees in summer sports, and all groups in winter sports)
National Headquarters
4405 East-West Highway, Suite 603
Bethesda, MD 20814
Tel: (301) 652-7505

United States Association for Blind Athletes (USABA)
33 North Institute Street
Brown Hall, Suite 15
Colorado Springs, CO 80903
Tel: (719) 630-0422

National Wheelchair Athletic Association (NWAA)
3617 Betty Drive, Suite S
Colorado Springs, CO 80907
Tel: (719) 597-8330

United States Cerebral Palsy Athletic Association (USCPAA)
34518 Warren Road, Suite 264
Westland, MI 48185
Tel: (313) 425-8961

United States Les Autres [the others] Sports Association (USLASA)
1101 Post Oak Boulevard, Suite 9-486
Houston, TX 77056
Tel: (713) 521-3737

Dwarf Athletic Association of
America (DWAA)
3725 West Holmes Road
Lansing, MI 48911
Tel: (517) 393-3116

American Athletic Association
of the Deaf (AAAD)
1052 Darling Street
Ogden, UT 84403

Other organizations:

National Amputee Summer
Sports Association (NASSA)
215 West 92nd Street,
Suite 15A
New York, NY 10025

Adolescent Sarcoma Patients'
Intense Rehabilitation with
Exercise (ASPIRE—for
amputees)
c/o Paddy Rossbach
196 East 75th Street
New York, NY 10021

Some annual athletic events for juniors with disabilities:

New York State Parks Games
for the Physically Challenged
Long Island Region
Belmont Lake State Park
P.O. Box 247
Babylon, NY 11702-0247
Tel: (516) 669-1000, ext. 294

The Ability Games of the
Junior Orange Bowl
5915 Ponce de Leon Boulevard
Plumer Building, 5th Floor
Coral Gables, FL 33146
Tel: (305) 284-4535

Acknowledgments

Special thanks to Peggy Guthart, my invaluable editorial assistant, who helped give shape to my transcripts, notes, and general observations; Carol Atkinson for her careful transcribing; Terry King for his good advice; Eugene Merinov for his excellent printing of my photographs; the gang at Simon & Schuster, particularly Fred Hills, Daphne Bien, and Burton Beals, who have been supportive, helpful, and nice; and my ever-congenial agent, Bob Tabian.

For helping to find the extraordinary children who appear in this book my appreciation to: Dr. Steve Hersh, Director of the Medical Illness Counseling Center in Chevy Chase, Maryland; Dr. Judy Wallin, Associate Professor of Clinical Pediatrics at the New York University School of Medicine; Dr. Marlene Wust at The New York Hospital–Cornell Medical Center; Paddy Rossbach; Dr. Leon Root; Arlene Gordon at The Lighthouse; Oscar Tang; George Gillette and Linda Tulenko of Vail Associates; Bob Baxter, President of the James Whitcomb Riley Memorial Association in Indianapolis; Dr. Kurt Hirshhorn, Chairman of Pediatrics, Mt. Sinai Medical Center in New York; and Dr. Robert Baehner, Chief of Pediatrics at Children's Hospital of Los Angeles. I am grateful to Billie Tisch, who took the time to drive me to Blythedale Children's Hospital, which is, I think, one of the finest facilities I've seen. Dr. Andrew Rothstein,

Superintendent of the Henry Viscardi School, was hospitable and helpful.

It was a pleasure to have my daughter Lily, age eight, accompany me on most of my interviews. Together, we visited Joey in Long Island and Krystle in the Bronx. We flew to Indianapolis for a few days at Camp About Face. We skied in Vail with Katherine and visited the Lowe family during the summer in Cape Cod. We spent a Saturday at The Lighthouse, watching Jacques d'Amboise teach his class for sight-impaired dancers. Our last outing was to Miami to visit with Michelle Fernandez and her family, during which time Lily and Michelle had a lot of fun bobbing around in the water. Lily loved the children and they loved her. More important, she was just good company for me.

When all is said and done, it is, of course, the children and their families who appear in the book to whom I, and I hope all of you, can be supremely grateful. They have opened their hearts and bared their souls in order to guide, and enlighten, all of us.

About the Author

JILL KREMENTZ is a photographer, journalist, and portraitist who has photographed and written more than two dozen award-winning books for young readers and adults. She was the 1984 recipient of *The Washington Post*/Children's Book Guild Nonfiction Award for "creatively produced works that make a difference." Her last book, *How It Feels to Fight for Your Life,* which was about chronic illness and disease, was the recipient of an Outstanding Science Book for Children award from the Children's Book Council and the National Science Teachers of America, and also the Joan Fassler Memorial Book Award from the Association for the Care of Children's Health. Ms. Krementz lives in New York City.